Charles Buchan's
ARSENAL
GIFT BOOK

selections from
CHARLES BUCHAN'S PUBLICATIONS
1951-73

Dear Reader,
As this is the first Gift Book which I have edited for you, I would like to
begin this little introduction by saying how much I hope you will enjoy the
stories and pictures which have been gathered together for you.

I expect many of you who are reading this are already old friends of
mine, boys who keep in touch with our greatest game through the columns
of "Football Monthly". But, whether we have already met, or whether we
are meeting here for the first time, I welcome you all, knowing how keen
you are on sport and how sound is your judgement.

Now it is your judgement that can help me. Let me know if you enjoy
this book - and if you do like it, tell your pals about it.

If, on the other hand, you have criticisms to make, let me know of them
and you can be sure I will do my very best to carry out your suggestions
when we publish this book in future years.

The idea has been to give you variety, to provide exciting reading, and
to print pictures which will capture highlights of the game and the great
footballers who make it so popular with us all.

I believe the recipe will be to your liking and hope that when you have
finished this volume you will begin to look forward to next year's!

Charles Buchan's introduction
to his first Soccer Gift Book, 1953–1954

Charles Buchan's Arsenal Gift Book
© Malavan Media and Football Monthly Ltd 2007

Malavan Media is a creative consultancy responsible for the
Played in Britain series of books and events
www.playedinbritain.co.uk

Edited by Simon Inglis
Text by Jon Spurling and Simon Inglis
Design by Doug Cheeseman and Jörn Kröger
Production by Jackie Spreckley
ISBN: 978 0 9547445 3 3
Printed by Zrinski, Croatia

Charles Buchan's
ARSENAL GIFT BOOK

Edited by
Simon Inglis

Introduction by
Jon Spurling

Published by Malavan Media

Cont

ents

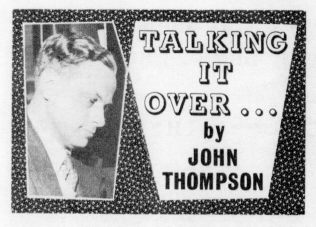

TALKING IT OVER . . . by JOHN THOMPSON

From the beginning . . .

AT first there was one chair in the office of "Football Monthly." I cannot remember why. We were hard-up for furniture for a long time. We would take it in turns to perch round a trestle table on orange boxes and would courteously leave the chair for any visitor who proved himself healthy enough to climb the steep stairs leading to our new home.

The trestle table was covered with a grey blanket and smelled of old apples. This was probably because Covent Garden was just round the corner.

Long before "Football Monthly" increased its tangible assets in any substantial way, Charles Buchan climbed the stairs with a purchase wrapped in brown paper. It was a splendidly expensive feather-duster.

Every morning Charles would whisk it energetically over the walls, the little pieces of furniture and the weary strips of linoleum.

Then he would look around as proudly as if he had just scored the winning goal against Scotland.

The moment he had finished, all the dust would settle down gracefully to await the next disturbance. The office overlooked the Strand, London . . . buses almost passed through the room, and it was difficult to keep clean for any time at all.

That first winter was singularly comfortless. In an unenviable spot, furthest from the windows, Joe Sarl would peer with a kind of hopeless determination at typescript and proofs and emerge at the end of the day with the lost look of a man who has been wandering through a thick fog.

He was, however, the warmest of our company.

To avoid frost-bite from the draughts that whistled through the room, Charles Buchan would wrap newspapers round his legs. The paper rustled disconcertingly whenever he moved.

LONG before winter fell, there had been the task of reading the first contributions to our first issue. There had been a fascinating incongruity in sitting on an orange box and studying the earliest article to arrive.

It came from that fine and kindly friend, the Marquess of Londonderry. He had been converted to Soccer by his friendship with miners in his father's pits.

There was a certain dream-like quality in reading Lord Londonderry's description of how he had become a director of Arsenal . . . because of a conversation over dinner at Buckingham Palace with the Master of the Horse, who happened to be Chairman of Arsenal.

Well, Buckingham Palace was only down the road from our office. And for a moment the bare electric light bulb was a candelabrum . . .

As this one hundredth edition of "Football Monthly" was being prepared, I glanced with nostalgia through that long-ago Number One.

The front cover picture was of Stanley Matthews, of Blackpool and England. **There could be no other choice, for Matthews has enriched the pleasures of us all and, in the years that have intervened, there has been no challenger for his place among the giants.**

Inside, were pictures of little Henry Cockburn, of Manchester United, and of Jimmy Dickinson, who has served Portsmouth with devoted loyalty through so many triumphs and disasters.

There, too, were bow-legged Joe Mercer and Mal Griffiths, the happy Welshman, and George Young leading out Scotland, and Jimmy Mason poised over the ball in the colours of Third Lanark. All were players remembered now with gratitude.

There, too, was Joe Harvey, telling with humility of the day Newcastle United won the F.A. Cup . . . *The King handed it to me and as he did so, I had the feeling that all the good people of Tyneside were with me . . . I felt that His Majesty was giving the Cup to me not as Joe Harvey, but as the representative of all those supporters, that I was getting it on their behalf.*

The Queen gave me my medal and I made my way down the steps, perhaps stumbling a little because I was near to tears . . .

TURN again the yellowing pages of that old "Football Monthly". Here is Raich Carter talking of bomb-battered Hull . . . *It was the success of Hull City Soccer team that helped to put Hull back on the map and restore the morale of people who had come to regard themselves as isolated and forgotten . . .*

Arthur Drewry, then Chairman of England's Selectors, told how *his imagination had been fired in Argentina and Brazil by the development of football grounds as first-class social centres; the centre-piece of the local community for every kind of recreative sport . . .*

Turn the pages . . . here is J. B. Priestley, capturing, as he did so well in "The Good Companions", the emotions of those who follow our greatest game . . . *It turned you into a member of a new community, all brothers together for an hour-and-a-half, for not only had you escaped from the clanking machinery of this less life, from work, wages, rent, doles, sick pay, insurance cards, nagging wives, ailing children, bad bosses, idle workmen, but you had escaped with most of your neighbours, with half the town, and there you were, cheering together, thumping one another on the shoulders, swopping judgments like lords of the earth, having pushed your way through a turnstile into another and altogether more splendid kind of life, hurtling with Conflict and yet passionate and beautiful in its Art . . .*

AND now, close the pages and consider for a moment how "Football Monthly" grew from its orange-box days into the voice of the greatest game man ever played, the game that spans frontiers with a handshake and knows no barriers of race or belief.

"Football Monthly" became a unique 'family affair'. Readers sent ideas and views on how to improve the magazine. Never had a publication received such friendly and loyal support.

The family was scattered, as the magic of football is scattered.

There was a boy in Brazil, a shoe-maker in Alaska, a judge's son in Yugoslavia, the skipper of a tug-boat who took two copies so that he could send one to an unknown kid in hospital.

There was a cinema manager in Australia, a cipher clerk in a British Embassy, a lance-corporal in the Malayan jungle.

The addresses from which they wrote ranged from Bolton to Burma. They came from destroyers and trawlers, factories and farms. Some were at village schools, others at Eton.

Thus did "Football Monthly" prosper because of the kindliness and understanding of its readers.

And it is the kindliness that will be remembered always— the gifts that readers asked us to send to sick children at Christmas, the gestures that helped old players down on their luck.

There were letters from prisons and mansions and there was the miracle of finding how blind people retain their love for football.

And the family grew and gained in strength and influence. It is loyal and sturdy, as it always was. We are very proud of it . . .

▲ December 1959

Foreword

by Simon Inglis
Played in Britain series editor

'Our object is to provide a publication that will be worthy of our National game and the grand sportsmen who play and watch it.'

For the discerning football fan of the 1950s and 1960s, *Charles Buchan's Football Monthly* was an absolute essential. If not for reading, then for the supply of bedroom posters.

Of course there were other publications on the market, such as the weekly *Sport* magazine, which ran until 1957, or *Soccer Star*, established in 1952. But neither had such bold design, such vibrant colour images, the collectability, the satisfying weightiness, nor any of the cameraderie that Charles Buchan and his team so knowingly infused into the pages of *Football Monthly*.

To be a reader of Charlie's magazine was to be a member of a fraternity.

In the world of Charles Buchan – a former Sunderland and Arsenal player known to millions for his match reports on BBC Radio – football was Soccer (always with a capital S), and Soccer was 'grand'. Indeed most things in Charlie's world were grand. The players were grand, the matches were grand, the footballing life itself was grand.

Buchan's magazine first appeared in September 1951 (when Charlie was already aged 61), just as the Festival of Britain was winding down on London's South Bank. Rationing was still in place. Paper was still in short supply. National Service was still obligatory for young men, while thousands of British troops were serving in Korea.

In the six years since Hitler's defeat, attendance levels at English football had soared to record levels, topping 41 million in 1948–49. Yet never before had the fortunes of the national team been so low, following England's humiliating defeat by the USA during the 1950 World Cup in Brazil (a match witnessed by Buchan and several of the Fleet Street veterans who would become his regular contributors).

Thus hope for the future, in the bright new world of post-war Britain, was necessarily tempered by anxiety concerning the health of the national game. Similarly, parochial pride in our footballing greats had always to be counterbalanced by reluctant admiration for the obvious skills of those 'Continentals' and 'Latins' from overseas. Hot-headed and devious they may have been, but clearly they had much to teach us, about tactics, training, even what kind of boots to wear.

So successful was *Charles Buchan's Football Monthly* that in July 1953 the publishers issued the first *Charles Buchan's Soccer Gift Book*. For the next two decades this jaunty annual earned an automatic slot on the Christmas wish lists of thousands of schoolboys.

Buchan himself, despite his reporting commitments with the BBC and the *News Chronicle* – whose staff he had joined in 1928 after retiring from Arsenal – remained actively involved in both publications until his death in June 1960, while on holiday in Monte Carlo. He was a tall man, always immaculately dressed and unfailingly polite. Columnist John Macadam, another writer of the old school, said of him, 'Charles sees only the good in all men.' But whereas Macadam and several of his fellow writers were hard drinking adventurers, Buchan retained the image of a schoolmasterly gent. And yet in his prime he had been both a supremely gifted and wily inside forward – his ratio of 224 goals in 413 games for Sunderland still stands as a record – and a brave soldier, winning a Military Cross during the First World War (a fact he modestly omitted from his autobiography, published in 1955).

By 1958 *Football Monthly's* circulation had risen to 107,000, at which point the offices moved from the Strand to 161-166 Fleet Street.

By a curious coincidence, this was the site of Andertons Hotel, where the Football League had formed in 1888. Not only that but the new building, Hulton House, was owned by the former publishers of *Athletic News*, once Britain's most popular football weekly.

After Charlie's death the proprietors kept his name on the masthead (until 1971), and under new editor Pat Collins – buoyed up by England's World Cup victory in 1966 – increased circulation to 200,000 in 1968. The following year it reached an all-time peak of 254,000. Membership of the Boys' Club topped 100,000.

Changing fashions may explain part of the magazine's demise in the early 1970s. As hairstyles lengthened and trousers grew more flared, more young readers were veering away from programme and autograph swaps in favour of records and pop-related memorabilia. Football itself was entering a period of decline, as the ravages of hooliganism began to take their toll on attendances.

Charlie's seemingly more innocent world was fading rapidly.

But also crucial was the decision by *Football Monthly's* new holding company, Longacre Press, to publish a sister magazine called *Goal*, in 1968. It took two years for *Goal* to outsell *Football Monthly*. Then a third contender materialised in the form of *Shoot*, a brash new weekly, published by IPC.

Shoot and *Goal* each sold over 220,000 copies weekly in 1971, compared with 164,000, and falling, for *Football Monthly*.

In August 1973 the publishers responded by rebranding the title in a smaller format. But as editor Pat Collins suspected, it was a losing battle, and in August 1974 the title left Fleet Street and became *Football Magazine*.

A golden era had truly passed.

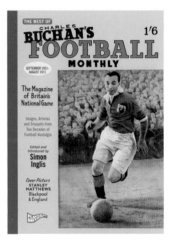

The compilation which follows is selected from issues of *Charles Buchan's Football Monthly* dating 1951–73, and from the *Charles Buchan's Soccer Gift Books,* published annually from 1953–74.

Inevitably readers will spot gaps; star players unmentioned, key events uncovered. Some of these omissions arise from lack of space. Others are simply owing to the fact that the magazine and gift books were by no means comprehensive in their coverage. If there is a narrative in what follows, therefore, it is fractured rather than cohesive, though hopefully no less appealing when viewed as a whole.

It will be noted that this book forms part of *Played in Britain*, a series which seeks to celebrate and preserve these islands' extraordinary sporting heritage.

Heritage is generally thought to reside in historic buildings, in places and landscapes. What it is hoped the following pages demonstrate is that there is heritage in ephemera too, and in the shared narrative that make us a nation, and a footballing nation at that.

For more on the Charles Buchan archive, see our list of related publications on the back page.

CLIFF HOLTON
Arsenal

Arsenal 1951–73

by Jon Spurling

When *Charles Buchan's Football Monthly* first hit the bookstands in September 1951, on the surface all seemed well in the Arsenal camp. Most of all, in the six years since the cessation of hostilities, the Gunners appeared to have successfully overcome almost all the problems they had faced when peacetime football finally resumed in 1946.

Not least of these was the state of Highbury. Part of the Clock End terrace had been deemed unsafe after a German bomb landed on the adjoining practice pitch in 1940. At the opposite Laundry End, later known as the North Bank, the roof had been completely destroyed by incendiaries. Starved of matchday income since 1939 – Arsenal decamped to White Hart Lane for the duration – by 1946 the club once dubbed 'the Bank of England team' were reported to have been more than £150,000 in debt.

Then there was the question of rebuilding the team. Most of the squad had lost their best playing days to the conflict, while pre war stars such as Ted Drake, Jack Crayston and Alf Kirchen would never play again, having sustained injuries during the war.

Facing the very real threat of relegation in the first post-war season of 1946–47, in November 1946 a worried Arsenal signed the 32 year old Everton wing half Joe Mercer, to be joined by the 33 year old Ronnie Rooke from Fulham.

Both cost only nominal fees. Herbert Chapman's claim in the early 1930s that Arsenal 'can afford to pay £2,000 more for a player than any other club' belonged to a bygone era.

In such straitened circumstances, all hope rested on Mercer's knees holding up, and on the club's bountiful youth policy yielding a quick crop of first teamers.

Meanwhile, after almost single handedly running the club throughout the war years, an exhausted George Allison, who had taken over the role after the death of Chapman in 1934, retired from the post of secretary-manager in May 1947.

Yet a year later, amazingly, Arsenal's patched up team won the League Championship. Newly revitalised off the field by Allison's successor, Tom Whittaker (the former club trainer), and on the field by Joe Mercer (whose leadership had a similar galvanising effect to that of Charles Buchan when he had signed for Arsenal in 1925), it appeared that the Gunners were now well on their way to recapturing the spirit of the 1930s.

This impression was further strengthened when Arsenal beat Liverpool 2-0 at Wembley to win the 1950 Cup Final.

Two seasons later the team promised even greater glories by finishing third in the League and reaching a second postwar Cup Final, lost by a single goal to Newcastle. Then a year later the League title returned to Highbury, albeit by the tiniest of margins. Come May 1953, Arsenal's goal average was just 0.099 superior to that of runners-up Preston.

Just as significantly, with the Highbury turnstiles regularly clocking up attendances of over 50,000, the club soon paid off its debts and, a month after the first issue of *Charles Buchan's Football Monthly*, became the first club in the top division to install floodlights.

By any other standards, these achievements should have erased all doubts as to the club's place in the rapidly modernising world of football.

But all was not as it seemed.

After a home defeat against Sunderland earlier in that Championship winning season of 1952–53, centre forward Peter Goring recalled a confrontation with a fan outside Highbury. 'This chap was completely drunk, but he started telling me that he'd seen the Arsenal team of the '30s, and we weren't fit to lick their boots. The ironic thing was that I agreed with the bloke. We were a battling team, rather than a side to be compared with the '30s vintage.'

Goring and his team-mates were given a further reminder of their place in Arsenal's hall of fame when one of the greatest icons of the 1930s, Alex James, died from lung cancer in June 1953. Although James had retired from playing in 1937 he had taken up coaching Arsenal's youth teams, and was a regular presence behind the scenes until his death, at the age of 51.

Even those who had never met or played alongside the Scot felt his loss keenly. Peter Goring recalled, 'To many of us, Alex James was Arsenal... and we knew that we were expected to live up to his side's massive achievements. It proved really hard. He almost became a kind of martyr. I had a fan come up to me and say, "Where is the next Alec James going to come from?"

'James and the 1930s Arsenal team were like ghosts haunting us every time we wore the shirt. And they carried on haunting all Arsenal players, until the early '70s really.'

Tommy Lawton, another cut-price veteran signed by Whittaker – from Brentford in September 1953 – felt the same.

'Many of the lads from the '30s always seemed to be on the scene. You'd have Ted Drake, the Compton brothers, Wilf Copping, and wee Alex when he was still alive, and George Male worked on the coaching staff. They'd hang around, and sometimes mix with us after the games. That didn't always go down too well with some of the lads. I remember Jimmy Logie asking why they couldn't "piss off down the pub and don't bore us with your memories".

'Other young players got fed up with being called the "new" whoever. I could see their point, but as a senior professional it was my job to point out to these lads that it was our responsibility to bring those good times back. It's hard though, when you can sense that things are in decline and won't change for the better for a while.'

One measure of Tom Whittaker's desperation to inject a spark of glamour was his attempt to sign yet another veteran, the Blackpool winger Stanley Matthews, probably the most famous player of his generation and the natural choice to appear on the cover of the first *Football Monthly*. According to one source, Whittaker first tried to sign Matthews in the summer of 1951, offering Blackpool manager Joe Smith a blank cheque, despite the player then being aged 32.

Three years later, as revealed in Matthews' autobiography of 2000, Whittaker tried again. Only this time he offered to double Matthews' wages by arranging a secondary job doing promotional work for a London catering company. In the days before the abolition of the maximum wage such an offer, though common enough, blatantly contravened League regulations.

Though tempted, Matthews turned Arsenal down. But it does illustrate both Whittaker's desire to bring a big name to Highbury, even one aged 35, and the fact that for all Arsenal's reputation as an outfit that did things by the book – a reputation frequently trumpeted in the pages of *Football Monthly* – if desperate, the club was no different from any other when it came to under-the-counter transfer dealings.

Not that they needed to offer incentives in every case.

September 1954

Doug Lishman, signed from Third Division Walsall in 1948, recalled that 'Arsenal officials were very clever, because in those days they couldn't blind you with talk of money, due to the maximum wage being in operation. But they could dazzle you with the inside of Highbury. It really was like a different world. The baths, the training facilities, the fact that the kit man washed and ironed your kit... you felt there was nowhere better to play football.'

Indeed the relative luxury of life at Arsenal proved a popular topic for players interviewed by *Football Monthly*.

Tommy Lawton recalled his arrival in 1953. 'From the outside the whole place really did need a lick of paint, but that was the case for a lot of London's major buildings. I did feel a pang of disappointment when I first saw the East Stand though. It had once been pristine, and had clearly fallen into a bit of a state. Inside, however, it was as palatial as ever.'

Joining Arsenal also brought with it the lure of adventurous tours, a tradition started by Herbert Chapman, the first British manager to advocate overseas air travel.

The images of Jimmy Logie and Alex Forbes on page 32 – at a time when many staples of everyday life were still subject to rationing – capture the essence of these foreign trips. As Doug Lishman recalled, 'Everything about travelling with Arsenal was first class. The club paid extra for waitress service on aeroplanes, and you'd be given lovely roasted meat, delicious puddings, cigars, ports, after dinner mints. Nothing was too much trouble. Although we may not have earned a fortune, we lived like kings, and were treated as such wherever we went. Can you imagine the excitement of travelling to South America as a 21 year old? It was

an experience which very few lads of my age would ever have. Arsenal was the first English club to really become a global name.'

Less appealing was the club's excursion to Moscow in 1956, at the height of the Cold War (featured on pages 34-35).

'It was a bizarre trip,' Tommy Lawton remembered, 'and I think quite a few of us had pangs of doubt from the minute we took off and saw the cabin crew's grim faces. The food on the trip was awful – we joked that the chicken soup we had when we got to Moscow still had the feathers on – and we constantly checked the rooms for bugging devices. At the time we didn't find it particularly funny, but you look back and think, well no one, basically, from the UK was allowed into Russia back then. But we saw the Kremlin and Red Square, and I still love the memories of that trip. We would never have gone there if we hadn't played for the Arsenal.'

For player after player featured on the pages of *Football Monthly*, signing for Arsenal was clearly the realisation of a dream.

Among many hopefuls was Gerry Ward ('the most exciting prospect at the club since Cliff Bastin' according to Tom Whittaker). After becoming Arsenal's youngest ever debutant at the age of 16, in August 1953, Ward recalls being 'crushed by expectation from the off. My debut went so well that straight away the press built me up into something I wasn't. After that, I was in and out of the side before I faded away.'

Also highly rated in their early careers were council worker Derek Tapscott, from Barry Town ('the new David Jack' according to the *Daily Mirror*), and from Leyton Orient, Vic Groves ('bearing similarities to Joe Hulme from the 30s' in the words of the Arsenal programme). Groves well remembers 'the pride I felt

when *Charles Buchan's Football Monthly* featured me after I joined. I remember the cameras being in my room at home, and my family made sure I had all my medals on show.'

In addition to the sheer pressure of expectation heaped upon those young shoulders, in the days of the maximum wage – which rose from £14 a week in 1951 to £20 by 1958 – there were also financial uncertainties, especially for those considering signing professional forms after their period of National Service. As Joe Haverty, an apprentice wire maker from Ireland, recalled years later, 'In some ways, deciding to play football for a career was the dodgiest decision of all. I'd imagine that for every one youngster who made it, there would be a hundred who'd regret the day they turned their back on a trade.'

In fact during the early 1950s it was usual for Arsenal to have nearly 60 full time professionals on their books. Inevitably, one by one, most faded into obscurity, hampered either by injuries (in the cases of Groves and Tapscott), or by a sinking realisation that they were simply not good enough. According to Gerry Ward, 'The only players in the '50s who were genuinely top drawer were Jimmy Logie and Jack Kelsey. The rest of us, in comparison, were nowhere near those two.'

For Tom Whittaker the constant strain of meeting expectations became overwhelming.

In his posthumously published autobiography, *Tom Whittaker's Arsenal Story* (see page 143) he admitted that in his darker moments 'I lay ill in bed, at times not caring whether I lived or died. The strain on my nerves had taken its toll...'

Eventually Whittaker collapsed from nervous exhaustion, and although he recovered and returned to the managerial hot seat, he died

in post, from a heart attack, in October 1956, aged 58. (Herbert Chapman had been 56 when he too had died in mid-season.)

'Let this be a warning to would be managers,' stormed the *Daily Mail*. 'The pressures of the modern game are often intolerable.'

Once again, Arsenal chose their next manager from within the club's ranks, promoting Whittaker's assistant, Jack Crayston. However, for the first time Crayston's duties did not include those of club secretary. Instead, that role fell to long term office assistant Bob Wall, whose own autobiography, *Arsenal from the Heart*, offers a fascinating insight into this period in the club's history (see page 143).

Fifth and twelfth place finishes in Crayston's two seasons in charge were hardly a disaster, but his most famous match in charge was the historic 5–4 home defeat against Manchester United. This was the Busby Babes' last match on English soil before the Munich air crash in February 1958.

Arsenal fan David White recalled, 'There was a 63,000 crowd that day at Highbury, but if we're being honest many of them turned up to see Duncan Edwards. Yes, the game was every inch as thrilling as the stories say, and there was none of the malice shown to United that we get today, but Arsenal lost, and that summed up the era. We were going right down the pan. In one game, we had Gordon Nutt and Danny le Roux in the team. We all used to say they sounded like a dodgy drag act.'

After Crayston the next former Arsenal stalwart to take up the managerial challenge, in July 1958, was the tough-talking George Swindin, who had not only won three League Championship medals as the Gunners' goalkeeper between 1937–54, but also spent four successful years as player-manager

"Isn't it amazing how lucky Arsenal are?"

▲ October 1951

▲ October 1957

with the up-and-coming non-League club, Peterborough United.

But once again, for all his forthright bluster, Swindin proved unable to rekindle the glory days.

As might be expected, Arsenal's decline was reflected both at the gate – with averages falling under 35,000 by 1960 – and by the relative paucity of articles on the club and its players during the period between the late 1950s and the late 1960s. Double winning neighbours Tottenham were now the north London darlings of the media.

But as our selection from the Charles Buchan archive shows, some events at Highbury were too newsworthy to ignore.

One in particular was the signing of striker George Eastham for £47,500 from Newcastle in 1960. Eastham had famously gone on strike at his previous club when they refused, as was their right under existing contractual regulations, to put him on the transfer list. Labelled by some as a martyr, for standing up for players' rights, and by others as a trouble-maker, his capture represented a huge gamble for Arsenal.

As Eastham later admitted, 'Every expensive Arsenal signing was regarded as a Messiah, who might prove the vital link to set them alight.'

Despite a scoring debut, inconsistent form soon led to the Arsenal crowd barracking him. Critics sneered at his 'butterfly tackling'. Then in late 1961, after the Professional Footballers' Association finally won its campaign to abolish the iniquitous maximum wage, Eastham turned down Arsenal's offer of £30 a week. In the *Islington Gazette* fans called him 'big-headed', 'greedy' and 'a symbol of all that's wrong with the English game' (even though Johnny Haynes at Fulham was earning £100 a week by that stage).

On the face of it, the board's appointment of squeaky clean, former England captain Billy Wright, as successor to Swindin in May 1962, seemed set to usher in a new era of glory. Even his marriage to Joy, one of the Beverley Sisters – British pop's leading female act of the 1950s – brought a smattering of glamour to the Gunners.

Despite his complete lack of managerial experience at club level, Wright gambled heavily on expensive signings, starting with a gigantic £70,000 for Torino's Joe Baker. With his Elvis quiff, ready smile and sharp play around the box, Baker became an instant crowd favourite. But as the 1962–63 season wore on, it became apparent that Eastham and Baker were incompatible as a strike force. Baker poached 31 goals that year. Eastham tucked away just four. 'We just kept getting in each other's way,' Baker admitted.

In one of Billy Wright's few successful tactical switches, Eastham moved to inside right, and for the next two years, with Alan Skirton, the 'Highbury Express,' providing the ammunition, the Baker–Eastham partnership flourished. Yet Arsenal continued to leak goals at the other end.

Wright's next major signing was the blond haired Ian Ure, from Dundee.The £62,500 fee was then a world record for a centre half.

Ure's debut was, in his own words 'utterly atrocious,' not that one would infer this from the magazine. Its photo caption of the match, at home to Wolves, failed to mention that the visitors' nippy forwards had darted around Ure like speedboats around an oil tanker, or that Arsenal lost 3-1. Indeed rarely did writers on *Charles Buchan's Football Monthly* sharpen their pens to criticise players. Almost invariably their tone was sympathetic, and seldom

controversial. But one contributor, the venerable Geoffrey Green of *The Times*, was not afraid to state the truth. In the Feburary 1964 issue he wrote baldly, 'Contemporary Arsenal do not measure up to the giants of the past.'

As Ian Ure later recalled, 'Billy Wright wasn't a good manager. He wasn't hard enough and didn't have the willpower to get the players to work together. Forwards played as forwards, and midfielders purely as midfielders. Some players simply played for themselves.'

Even Frank McLintock, another expensive Wright signing – from Leicester City in November 1964 – complained that 'Billy relied on big name players too much.'

Nor did a change in the playing strip yield any benefits. At the start of the 1965–66 season the club abandoned the characteristic white sleeves that Herbert Chapman had introduced in 1932, so that Arsenal's all-red shirts with white cuffs and necks were now identical to a host of other teams (as shown in the team group on page 85).

Traditionalists assumed that Billy Wright was behind this controversial move, as it was well known that the beleaguered manager regularly shook his fist at the bust of Chapman which sat in pride of place in Highbury's 'marble hall' entrance. In fact, many years later Frank McLintock admitted that the idea had been his. But for hard core Gunners fans it was all the proof they needed. Clearly, Billy Wright was not 'an Arsenal man'.

Wright's lowest point arrived on the night of May 5 1966, nine weeks before the start of the World Cup, when just 4,554 spectators turned up at Highbury to see the Gunners take on Leeds United in a relatively meaningless end of season match. True, the weather that night was poor, and Liverpool's European Cup Winners' Cup Final against

Borussia Monchengladbach was being broadcast live on television. Even so, never had such a pitiful crowd attended a First Division match at Highbury.

On the nearly deserted North Bank a group of fans lit a bonfire and amused themselves by dancing around it for the entire second half.

Arsenal supporter Billy Hayes recalls, 'He was a nice guy – Billy Wright. But he was a disaster for Arsenal. There were loads of pictures of him with Joy Beverley in their stupid outfits. We were a bloody laughing stock. On a couple of occasions boycotts were arranged for games. It was rough to be honest. You'd hear chants of "Wright out, Wright out." I don't think I'd ever heard that sort of thing at Highbury before.'

Gunners fan Rory Hinds adds, 'By now, the maximum wage had been abolished. These guys were on good money, and we expected them to perform.'

So it was that while 1966 was a great year for England, for Arsenal, finishing fourteenth in the League – their lowest ranking since 1930 – and with average gates slumping to below 30,000 for the first time since the 1920s, it was an *annus horribilis*. Unsurprisingly Billy Wright left during the summer, to further his career in television, while the club reverted to its former practice by appointing his successor from within the club's ranks.

Sceptics feared that club physiotherapist Bertie Mee would struggle in the post of manager, an attitude echoed by the magazine's Peter Morris in an unusually analytical article in the October 1968 issue. Will Arsenal really mean something this season, he asked, noting that Frank McLintock and Jon Sammels had both requested transfers. And yet within the Highbury camp there lay the seeds of a remarkable revival, and ▶

one which would ultimately feature several of the youngsters, such as Jon Sammels, John Radford, Peter Storey and Charlie George, signed during Billy Wright's tenure, together with Mee signings George Graham from Chelsea and Bobby Gould from Coventry. (Interestingly, in view of the modern day Arsenal squad, Morris also alluded to the fact that Mee's squad included only four London born players, and intriguingly, one from Accra, in Ghana. Records reveal the latter to have been a triallist called P. Addo, of whom nothing more is known.)

In time McLintock was won over by the new manager. 'Bertie was actually very forward thinking, in contrast to the stuffy sergeant-major image that most people had of him. He wasn't a great coach by any means, but he knew that Don Howe was, and let Don get on with that side of things, whilst he shaped the squad, axed older players, and gave youngsters their chance. The main thing was that Bertie was given time by the board to bring in fresh blood, and re-energise the club.'

At last, in 1969 Arsenal seemed set to win their first trophy for 16 years, after reaching the League Cup Final. With Swindon their opponents, assistant editor Pat Collins was not alone in claiming 'It will be Arsenal's This Time.' Yet on a Wembley pitch churned up by the Horse of the Year Show, the Gunners were thumped 3-1.

'I remember talking to the magazine after the game,' recalls McLintock, 'and I was absolutely shattered. The picture (page 97) sums up my mood perfectly. I was so distraught because this was the fourth time I'd lost at Wembley, and I ended up getting tangled up with the marching band. It's a powerful picture because not only does it sum up my feelings at the time, but the tabloids also got hold of it, twisted it, and said things like

"Once more, Arsenal have lost their way." The *Evening Standard* ran a story beginning "Arsenal – The Shame Of London," and that acted as a huge kick up the backside.'

Within twelve months Arsenal lifted their first trophy since 1953, after defeating Anderlecht in the 1970 European Fairs Cup Final.

Interviews with Ray Kennedy and Charlie George confirm the impact this victory had on the club, and nearly forty years later, the 3-0 home win is still recalled with awe.

'You'd see pictures of the 1930s side all around the stadium, and it made you feel inadequate, to be honest,' recalls goalkeeper Bob Wilson. 'We had to strive to achieve what they did. There were pictures of the Mercers, the Drakes, and all the others, and someone suggested taking those pictures down. But Don Howe always argued that we had to be aware of their achievements, in order to try and match them.'

Goals by Eddie Kelly, John Radford and Jon Sammels won Arsenal the trophy, but already, McLintock had his eye on bigger prizes. 'I think we all realised that Arsenal was awake again, and that the millstone had been lifted. We believed this could be the start of something massive for Arsenal.'

As indeed it was. The highlights of the Gunners' historic 1970-71 Double winning season have been written about in numerous Arsenal histories, and the abiding images – Kennedy's header at White Hart Lane to secure the League title, Storey's equalising penalty at Hillsborough in the FA Cup Semi Final, and Charlie George's 'Jesus Christ Superstar' celebration after scoring the winner against Liverpool in the Cup Final – are all captured in *Football Monthly*.

After the Double had been won, Frank McLintock recalled one elated team mate informing an Arsenal

director to 'stick your Alex James'.

The ghosts of Arsenal's glorious past, which haunt most of the pages of this book, appeared finally to have been exorcised.

Between 1971 and the magazine's departure from Fleet Street in 1974, football underwent a number of changes.

Arsenal's opening home game of the 1971–72 season, a 4-0 win against Manchester United, was the club's first home game to appear in colour on *Match Of The Day*.

Young Gunners Peter Marinello and Charlie George were beginning to branch out into modelling and music. As wages rose, players grew warier of speaking to the press.

Charlie George explains, 'The tabloids were getting bolder and bolder and more pushy and muck raking. The stories they ran were often trivial – like they focused on my hair – or tried to stir up trouble. Players started to watch what they said to the press, and if they did speak, they demanded a fee. Not huge amounts of course, but some magazines wouldn't pay.

'I grew up enjoying *Charles Buchan's Football Monthly*, and I was happy to talk to them. But I'd hold back, and only really spill the beans, with, say a real red top. I'd never have dreamed of telling *Football Monthly* about my problems with Bertie Mee, but I would to a tabloid hack who was paying for it. It was a shame, but Charlie's mag was starting to seem a bit outdated.'

Our final extract in this collection – taken from *Charles Buchan's Soccer Gift Book* for 1973–74 – features the arrival at Arsenal of World Cup winner Alan Ball, for a British record fee of £220,000, from Everton in late 1971.

Ball's driving enthusiasm drew plaudits from team mates. But his arrival also symbolised the growing player power in the game. The

fussy, stiff upper-lipped Bertie Mee was already struggling with Charlie George's 'problem boy' image, while Ball was not afraid to tell Mee on numerous occasions that he disagreed with his tactics. Ball was also happy to be photographed by tabloid newspapers gambling his (then) gargantuan wages. He even advocated setting up The Clan, an exclusive group of footballers – consisting of the likes of Geoff Hurst, Stan Bowles and Alan Hudson – to exploit their marketing potential.

Rather like Arsenal, the idea fell flat in the mid 70s. But the fact that Ball was willing to push for lucrative deals outside football seemed a million miles from Jimmy Logie's claim in the early 1950s that 'the maximum wage ensures that players work for the love of the game, rather than the pursuit of money'.

Then again, had anything changed? Joe Mercer had run a grocers in order to supplement his football wage, while Charlie Buchan himself ran an outfitters in Sunderland, which doubled his weekly wage.

But for sure one thing had changed irrevocably.

Football Monthly failed to obtain an interview with Alan Ball for one simple reason. Shortly before his untimely death in 2007 he explained, 'When a player with a profile like mine moved club, you'd have everyone from the press buzzing around you. But I'm afraid that because the magazine didn't pay a fee, they wouldn't get a look in with big stars anymore.'

So it was that as the magazine ran out of steam and Arsenal finally rediscovered their sparkle, the world of football moved on, leaving other, better funded and more fashionable publications to pick up Buchan's mantle. In publishing, as in football, what counted was results.

THAT WONDERFUL MOMENT WHEN—"THE CUP IS OURS"

Joe Mercer's grin reflects all the joy of success as he clutches sport's most treasured Trophy after Arsenal's defeat of Liverpool

▲ May 1952

Only the ignorant think they know it all

Joe Mercer introduces Jimmy Logie to the Prime Minister before the kick-off of the Cup Final at Wembley.

IT had never occurred to me that there could be such pride in being captain of a losing team.

But when I led Arsenal away after Newcastle United's Cup Final win at Wembley I felt as much honour at being associated with this great bunch of "fighters" as I had ever felt in a winning side.

And now looking back on that unforgettable day I find it curiously linked in my mind with a remark which Leslie Compton made to me once. He told me : "Joe, you've been an Arsenal player all your life without knowing it ! "

It was one of the kindest compliments I have ever received, and it set me wondering : "What makes an Arsenal type of footballer ? "

The answer is not easy to explain, but I believe it is based largely on the conviction that the club is far greater than anyone in it, whether they are directors, manager or players.

So many clubs seem to revolve round one or two men. That is not so at Arsenal, for the club has had the good fortune to have a continuity of ideas and method, due to the single-mindedness of such managers as Herbert Chapman, George Allison and Tom Whittaker.

There has been no interruption to the building of the Arsenal tradition.

Even when I was an Everton player I found that the tag "lucky Arsenal" was unjustified. **It was not luck. It was method.**

I soon realised that the method was not easily come by. It had to be worked for.

And it depended enormously on one factor which I discovered very quickly— the assurance that if one player is having a bad time there is always someone to rally round and to ease him over it.

These points Arsenal have taught me. Yet, looking back on my long career in the game, I cannot help but reflect how much there still is for me to learn.

I am certain that it is only the fellow with little experience and limited knowledge who knows " the lot " and believes that everything is easy.

No one could ever justly claim to know all there is to know about such a contradictory and complex game.

Just listen to acknowledged authorities discussing a team. Note how their opinions vary about its rights and wrongs.

Who is to say, dogmatically, that one or the other is correct ?

Consider, too, the elementary needs of a good player. See how they contradict each other : The player must retain his individuality and play in his own natural way. He should not conform to type and must do the unexpected.

Yet he must sink his individuality to conform to the good of the team and not play well at a team-mate's expense or do anything which might mislead his colleagues.

I expect there are many ways of reconciling all those points, but the man who imagines that *his* particular way is the one and only way is in for a lot of trouble.

Incidentally, how I hate the expression "tactical." I would substitute the phrase: "Common sense."

And that digression takes me a stage farther in this chat about football philosophy—"**One ounce of experience is worth a ton of theory.**"

There is certainly quite enough trouble just in playing football without adding fantastic theoretical talk. The more simple, the more direct and straightforward we are the more successful we will be.

What a wealth of wisdom and experience are condensed into Matt Busby's statement: "**THE EASY THING QUICK !**"

The only tactics which have any appeal to me are those gained by experience of actually playing football.

Object of a good coach, in my view, should be: "How little can I say? Not how much."

But don't get the impression from this that I am anti-coaching altogether. I do feel that it has its place in the game, although I would not rank it so importantly as some of those in "high places" would.

I *am* sure that the best time and place for coaching is while a match is in progress. As proof of this argument I offer for your consideration the work of men such as Peter Doherty, of Doncaster Rovers, and Raich Carter, of Hull City.

Think how valuable to younger members of their teams the advice and example of Doherty and Carter must have been.

The game has always had and always will have its outstanding characters, men who by their natural leadership and personality do the job of player-manager unconsciously.

" My wife says horizontal stripes make me look fat."

Throughout football history there have been these men who *taught as they played*, men such as Warney Cresswell, Frank Barson, Jock Thompson.

My advice to youngsters who are fortunate to be playing alongside stars of this calibre (and the name Jimmy Hagan comes immediately to mind) is to digest all the knowledge they can pass on to you.

Be honest with yourself if you are criticised. The reason will probably be there for you to see if you have the sense to recognise it.

There are, I know, some older players who criticise youngsters to cover up their own shortcomings. There are some who haven't the knack of imparting advice during the heat of a game, and only antagonise their team-mates.

Here again, experience must be the only guide for you to decide which is the "genuine article."

I know that in my own early days, in the star-studded Everton side, there were several outstanding players who gave us youngsters confidence in ourselves.

Their exceptional skill and fitness set a standard which was just the incentive we required . . .

And even to-day I can see in Tommy Lawton many of the mannerisms and tricks of Billy Dean . . .

ARSENAL, Champions of the Football League. Back row: Daniel, Milton, Goring, Kelsey, Forbes, Roper. Front row: Wade, Logie, Mercer, Smith, Lishman. Insets: Swindin, Holton, Shaw.

▲ August 1953

JIMMY LOGIE
Arsenal

MEMORY LANE

MANY of us this season will miss the company of Alex James. The little man, with the long baggy pants, has seen his last game.

He will always be remembered for his brilliant play at inside-left for Scotland and Arsenal. His trick with the " fluttering foot " that bewildered so many opponents, is copied even to-day.

There are still many youngsters who, during their school play and practice, want to be Alex James.

But despite many wonderful performances, including his part in Scotland's Wembley Wizards, in 1928, and the F.A. Cup winning goal against Huddersfield Town, in 1930 final, I prefer to regard Alex as a schemer and tactician, an unruffled leader, who, no matter whether his side were winning, losing or drawing, went on playing the game in his inimitable way.

His influence on the rest of his colleagues was incalculable.

Arsenal, during their triumphant period in the early 1930s, owed a great deal to the imperturbability of the perky little Scot with the twinkling eyes and sense of humour.

Though the target of close attention from opponents, James never lost his poise. He went on with the ball jugglery, inspiring his team-mates by his own example.

He thought quickly, too. I remember in one game, when Arsenal were having so much of the play that the ball was hardly ever out of the opponents' half, James sent a long pass back to his goalkeeper from near the half-way line.

The idea was to entice the defenders away from their goal and give Arsenal the chance to bring off one of their often successful " smash-and-grab " raids.

Never was the coolness and courage of James better defined than during Arsenal's F.A. Cup semi-final with Hull City, at Elland Road, in 1930, the year they won the Cup for the first time.

Hull, a Second Division side, had established a two-goal lead in the first half, the second goal, an extraordinary one, scored by inside left Jimmy Howieson direct from a goal-kick by goalkeeper Dan Lewis.

A GRAND FELLOW

Hull were on top, Arsenal ragged and dispirited. But James, as cool as ever, rallied the side by his clever ball play. Soon after the interval David Jack reduced the arrears, and then, as the minutes were flying fast, and the end approaching, James slipped a beautiful through pass to his partner, Cliff Bastin.

The outside-left took the ball on the run and crashed it, from just outside the penalty area, into the Hull net. Arsenal, thanks to James and Bastin, had pulled the game out of the fire.

In the replay, at Villa Park, the following Wednesday, tempers became ruffled. There were many unsavoury incidents which culminated in a Hull half-back being ordered off the field by the referee.

Through all the bitter exchanges, James remained calm and unruffled. Eventually his sterling work was rewarded.

He made a splendid opening for inside-right David Jack to score the only goal of the game.

Then, of course, there was the first goal in the final with Huddersfield, at Wembley. James had been brought down by a defender.

Quickly he seized the ball, placed it on the spot, and, without wasting any time, slipped the ball to Bastin. Back came the ball instantly for James to send an 18-yards shot hurtling into the Huddersfield net.

James also made his influence felt in the pre-match tactical talks. There was one Arsenal meeting at which there had been much discussion around a field with miniature players moved about to emphasise the points.

When it came to James's turn to speak, he swept the players, with one movement of his arm, off the field on to the floor, with the remark : " There's another team besides Arsenal playing."

I remember Ivor Broadis, England inside-right, saying to me : " When I was a 16-year-old with Spurs, Alex James taught me a lot. He was a grand fellow."

That is the general opinion—a grand fellow whose place will be hard to fill. Both England and Scotland could do with one like him.

CHARLES BUCHAN.

◄ November 1951 | September 1953 ▲

▲ November 1953

▲ May 1953

EVERY inside-forward will agree with me that the loss of his wing partner through injury during a match is a blow.

It usually means handling the entire wing single-handed—and tactical ideas have to be adjusted to meet the new situation.

Next to injury to himself, I suppose it's the worst thing that can happen to an inside-forward. **Yet such a circumstance paved the way for my own entry into big football.**

I was playing in a Cup final for Lochore Welfare, in Fifeshire junior football, and Arsenal's representative was there to watch me.

I felt my chances of making a good impression were down to zero when my wing partner was taken off injured.

But, strange to relate, it proved my golden opportunity.

With two positions to fill, I had more of the play than usual and, as good luck would have it, the ball was running for me.

Arsenal's scout saw enough of me in that game to send a satisfactory report to Highbury.

I've always felt that the injury to my Lochore partner was instrumental in launching me into League football.

That's how Arsenal came to sign me, but I must not forget the part played by a certain Mr. Parker, a barber in Dunfermline.

"ARSENAL HEARD ABOUT DUNFERMLINE BARBER"

He used to watch the Lochore Welfare team and, confident that I would make the professional grade, he wrote to Arsenal suggesting they should take a look at me.

The day I signed for Arsenal was, I suppose, the proudest of my life.

But joining the paid ranks of a famous League club merely signalises the start of a young player's efforts.

I remember how awestruck and insignificant I felt when I reported at Highbury during the summer of 1939.

No ground anywhere in football is quite so impressive to the newcomer as Arsenal Stadium and to find oneself, as a raw youth, amid players of world renown, like Eddie Hapgood and Bryn Jones, was enough to set my pulse racing.

I came under the immediate supervision of Jack Lambert, then looking after the " A " team.

Both he and Herbert Roberts did a lot to ease my feeling of strangeness in those early days.

Arsenal's third team figured in the Southern League at that time, playing home matches on the ground of Enfield, the Athenian League club.

It was there that I played my only match for the club before the war stopped big football in the second week of the season.

That first game, comparatively unimportant as it was, remains much more vividly impressed upon my mind than many of the big Cup and League battles in which I have since played.

We won the match, against Worcester City, by 3—1, and all our goals were scored by Tom Whalley, who afterwards faded out of football.

So, when I joined the Navy two months later, I was an Arsenal player—but only just. I had had one game in their colours to my credit.

Naval service provided me with plenty of opportunities for playing football and at one time, I was playing six games a week !

I wasn't so fortunate towards the time of my demobilisation, and I recall an occasion when I was free to play for Arsenal.

It was early in 1946, and as the club had a settled team at the time, I was asked to fill a gap as a guest in the Plymouth Argyle team visiting the Spurs.

I played inside-left, but hadn't had a match for months.

Spurs beat us 2—0, and at the finish I felt all-in. I know Plymouth people won't recall my display that day with any relish.

But let me get back to my school-days in Edinburgh.

I attended Castle Hill School, in the shadow of Edinburgh Castle, and never missed a chance of playing football.

The light evenings meant extra football and we were always kicking about in the " back courts "—as we call them in Scotland.

Jimmy Logie . . . he once played in goal !

▲ March 1953

ME FROM A

I never lacked companions. I have five brothers and although none of them took football as seriously as I did, they were always ready to join in.

My ambition as a schoolboy was to play for Hearts. I went to Tynecastle regularly and my idol in those days was Tommy Walker, who now manages the club.

Tommy's position was the same as mine and I watched his every move.

Another great Hearts player who captured my imagination was Alex Massie. He captained Scotland from right-half and was transferred to Aston Villa in 1935.

George Stevenson, the Motherwell inside-left, was another Scottish player who commanded my respect.

My enthusiasm for Hearts landed me in trouble on one occasion.

Dundee were visiting Tynecastle for a big match, in mid-week and, with two friends, I decided that just that once, school could be given the by-pass in favour of Hearts.

Hearts were in great form and won 4—0. But we were on the carpet at school next day. Luckily, the teacher concerned was a good sport and did not take too serious a view of our offence.

That smile on Logie's face was caused by the news that he'd been capped for Scotland against Ireland.

My ambition to become a Hearts player was never realised. I was allowed to train on the Tynecastle ground as a boy and thought I might receive an invitation to play for the club.

But it never came. I think my small physique was the reason.

My shortness didn't seem to matter so much in schools' football. Perhaps it was because the rest of our team was small.

Believe it or not, but in my first match in proper football kit as a schoolboy, I played in goal !

But it was the first and only time I had that job. I let the ball go through my legs into the net ! Team-mates don't easily forget a thing like that !

I had a thorough apprenticeship in junior football with Lochore. It was a hard school, but it sharpened my Soccer wits.

On one occasion we were playing a Cup-tie at a mining village in the Lothians. We beat the locals, much to the chagrin of the crowd, and for our audacity were chased off the ground by the mob.

I'm not naming the village—I may need to go there again some time !

Looking back over my years with Arsenal, I know that nothing has equalled the tremendous thrill I felt when Reg Lewis scored our first goal, from my pass, against Liverpool in the Wembley final of 1950.

But not far behind that precious moment was an occasion late in season 1947-48.

We were playing Burnley, at Highbury, and like us, they were after the championship. We beat them 3—0, staved off formidable challengers and went on to win the title.

The abiding memory of that game was a brace of brilliant goals by Ronnie Rooke.

You may expect me to mention my first League game for Arsenal. Well, it was uninspiring.

It was at Wolverhampton, at the end of August, 1946, and I played at inside-left. The first half was goalless, but the Wolves turned on the heat after the break, and we finished 6—1 losers.

So it was my privilege (?) to figure in one of Arsenal's worst defeats.

On the following Wednesday we met Blackburn Rovers, at Highbury, and suffered another defeat. But a boil in the ear kept me out of the side until the following Saturday, when I replaced George Drury against Sunderland.

Harking back to those early post-war games, I recall an uncomfortable but perhaps enlightening, experience.

In that first post-war season Arsenal's team was undergoing reconstruction and the experiment was tried of playing me at left-half.

I played four matches in that position and one of them I shall never forget.

It was against Derby County. I found myself opposed to two inside-forwards. Or, that's how it seemed !

Derby's inside-right was Raich Carter, but he switched places so frequently with Peter Doherty, the inside-left, that I was left in a whirl.

Was I glad to get back to that inside-forward position !

I've been fortunate to spend my career with Arsenal. I can't compare conditions at Highbury with those elsewhere because I've never been on the staff of another club.

But no club could do more for its players than Arsenal, and I've always been very happy at Highbury.

Only disappointment of my football life is that I never saw Alex James in action.

What a player he must have been !

LIONEL
SMITH
Arsenal
and
England

A graphic study of all-out effort—snapped in TOM LAWTON'S first game for Arsenal following his transfer from Brentford. Lawton (left) is in a tussle with Manchester City goalkeeper Bert Trautmann and centre-half David Ewing.

◀ April 1953 | November 1953 ▲

SPOTLIGHT ON
ARSENAL

ARSENAL, called by some "Lucky Arsenal," by others the "Bank of England" team, are the most hated, yet the most respected team in Britain.

Most hated for their tremendous successes in the past 30 years. Every team is out to beat them. Yet they are the most respected because of the immense good they have done for the game.

For years now, every game has been a Cup-tie for Arsenal players. Every team they have met has pulled out that little extra against the champions.

But that has not stopped their triumphant progress. In 28 years—actually, 20 playing seasons, because the second World War intervened—they brought off a series of performances unsurpassed in the game and unlikely to be equalled in the future.

During that time they won the League championship six times—a record equalled only by Aston Villa and Sunderland—equalled Huddersfield Town's record breaking feat of winning the title three years in succession, won the F.A. Cup three times, at Wembley, established crowd records at several League grounds, and at Arsenal Stadium.

In short, made themselves the outstanding team of the era.

And then last season they had the triumph of winning their seventh championship.

Success has brought fame and made them the wealthiest club in the land. They have made enormous profits since the war. But it was not always like that. Quite the reverse in fact.

Three times during their career, which began in 1886, Arsenal have nearly put up the shutters.

The first time was in 1891, when, after a successful period in local competitions, they took the plunge into professionalism, the first Southern club to do so, under the name Woolwich Arsenal.

They were boycotted by the rest of the Southern clubs for their bold venture. They could fix up only "friendlies" with Northern and Midland teams. When they tried to found a League of Southern teams, nobody took any notice of them.

In desperation, they applied, in 1893, for admission to the Football League. Luckily for them they got it.

It was a lucky break for a team that owed its beginning to men from Nottingham Forest, who had gone to work in Woolwich Arsenal.

They were the mainstays of the first amateur side. At one time, they persuaded Forest to let them have a set of red jerseys. That is how they came to get the present colours.

The second time Woolwich Arsenal escaped disaster was during the Boer War.

Most of their supporters were either soldiers, or arsenal workers, and had not the time for such things as football matches at the Manor Field—Arsenal's first League ground.

Only the generosity of a local business man saved the club from bankruptcy.

The third, and last, time was in 1908, when the late Sir Henry Norris and Mr. W. Hall, both Fulham directors, joined the Woolwich Arsenal board.

After five years' hard struggling for survival, they decided to transport the club from the Manor Field to the present palatial Highbury quarters.

From that day, in 1913, all financial difficulties have been smoothed away.

After a season at Highbury, Woolwich was dropped from the name. It became plain Arsenal. And they had the name of the underground railway station immediately outside the ground changed from Highbury to Arsenal.

They were in the Second Division then. After the first World War, Arsenal were elected to the First Division when it was extended. They did not have to win promotion.

For six years they jogged along near the bottom, just avoiding relegation—until 1925, when the great Herbert Chapman, who had piloted Huddersfield to their wonderful achievements, was appointed manager.

That was the year when the offside law was changed. It was the turning point. Under Chapman's guidance, Arsenal outstripped all rivals.

New tactics, which revolutionised the game, and brought forth Herbert Roberts,

Jimmy Logie and Doug Lishman (left), read a report of their match. Above, George Swindin gives a big smile from the bath.

▲ June 1953

Skipper Joe Mercer slices the bacon in his grocer's shop at Hoylake.

Prince of "stopper" centre-halves, were introduced and paid handsome dividends.

Roberts was the king-pin around whom a great team was built. Arsenal spent money to get the best players available.

David Jack, Alex James, Joe Hulme, Tom Parker, Jimmy Dunne, and many others, were brought to Arsenal Stadium at a huge cost. No expense was spared to make them the supreme team.

It was a very expensive, but highly successful business. It brought the nickname " Bank of England " team to a side that years before had not known how to make ends meet.

The other League clubs could have no complaint. For it was Arsenal who proposed at a League meeting that transfer fees for players should be limited to £1,650. They turned down the proposal and Arsenal became the biggest spenders of their time.

A record £10,340 for David Jack, from Bolton Wanderers, another record £14,000 for Bryn Jones, Wolverhampton Wanderers, inside-left, and other big cheques for first-class players, kept Arsenal at the top of the tree.

★

It was said at one period that Arsenal's methods were negative and took the beauty out of the game. But they were eminently profitable.

Arsenal supplied the thrills, the excitement and the glamour that the public wanted—and flocked to see.

Arsenal's methods brought them many imitators, but few teams had players of the calibre of the inimitable Alex James, the ice-cool international Cliff Bastin, and the thunderbolt Ted Drake.

Certainly, no other team found such a " Rock of Gibraltar " defence as that put up by goalkeeper Frank Moss and full-backs George Male and Eddie Hapgood.

Even after the sudden death of the great Herbert Chapman, Arsenal, under the management of George Allison, continued to be the League's biggest attraction until the start of the second World War, when their stadium was closed down and they shared Tottenham Hotspur's ground at White Hart Lane.

There was a time after the war when Arsenal were on the verge of a depression.

At one time they were threatened with relegation.

But newcomers, like Joe Mercer, from Everton, and Ronnie Rooke, of Fulham, soon restored them to their old pre-eminence.

But now that Tom Whittaker—who has been with the club as player and trainer—is manager, Arsenal are no longer the top price experts.

Their biggest fee ever, £15,000, was paid for Alex Forbes, the Scottish international half-back, of Sheffield United. They refuse to be stampeded into the £30,000 class.

Arsenal's record since the war testifies to the soundness of their policy and the judgment of their officials.

They were League champions in 1948, F.A. Cup winners in 1950, and have built a reputation second to none on the Continent and in South America for their great displays of Soccer craft and sportsmanship.

Arsenal have done a lot for the good of the game and they are likely to go on doing it for many years to come.—C. B.

Followed by Jim Logie Mercer leads out Arsenal.

Joe Wade obliges with autographs for eager schoolboy fans.

It was a good kick-off for Queen's Park Rangers in the first floodlit match to be played on their ground. Spotlight was on stage star Pat Kirkwood, who is watched by Arsenal's Don Roper (left) and Joe Taylor, of Queen's Park Rangers.

JOE WADE
Arsenal

CHARLES BUCHAN'S FOOTBALL MONTHLY

1/6

MARCH 1953

RAY DANIEL of Arsenal . . . **STANLEY MATTHEWS** of Blackpool

THE FRONT DOOR TO FAME . . .

The imposing front entrance of the most palatial Soccer ground in Britain.

IT is an ordinary-looking green filing-cabinet, pushed against the wall of a neat office in Arsenal Stadium. And in it there are a thousand ambitions . . .

Ask Jack Crayston, Arsenal's assistant-manager, to pull open one of the drawers and he will show you heaps of letters which have come from boys who want to play for Arsenal.

Wherever they come from, all are carefully examined, investigated and filed away. In many cases, where there is a definite hint of latent promise, one of the club's scouting staff is sent to watch the boy who has brought himself to Highbury's notice.

What happens then? Well, the scout may be impressed by the boy's play. In that case manager Tom Whittaker may get a letter from him something on these lines: "I have watched John Blank and feel that he might be an Arsenal type. He comes from a good home and I have had a chat with his parents. It is probable that he will agree to sign for Arsenal although other clubs are interested in him . . ."

At seventeen he is old enough to become a professional. But even so his parents may be reluctant to let him leave home. Often it happens that Mr. Whittaker sends an understanding letter to the lad's father in which he invites both father and son to visit the ground. When they come they are shown around Highbury, the dressing-rooms and the gymnasium, and the lodgings where the lad will stay.

Mr. Whittaker explains the care with which the boy will be looked after, emphasises that he

One of Arsenal's young "hopefuls," Raymond Swallow, signs professional forms in the Highbury office of assistant-manager Jack Crayston. He then goes on a "conducted" tour of Arsenal Palace.

▲ 1953–54 Gift Book

IF YOUR NAME IS IN THE . . . .

will be encouraged to save his wages and, if he wishes, continue his studies.

Content that his future will be a happy one, the young professional is taken downstairs. He meets the famous players whom he may have last seen close-up when he sought their autographs.

Later he is handed two tickets for each game—and, far more important, a slim book with a red cover—the Arsenal code of conduct.

Jack Crayston will doubtless tell his young charge that the most important section comes near the end. Here it says: "You are an Arsenal player. It should be a point of honour with you to conduct yourself in a manner which will ensure your taking the field in a perfect balanced mental and physical

condition, thus enhancing your own and the club's reputation . . ."

You are an Arsenal player. The pride in that little phrase is the secret of Arsenal's greatness . . . .

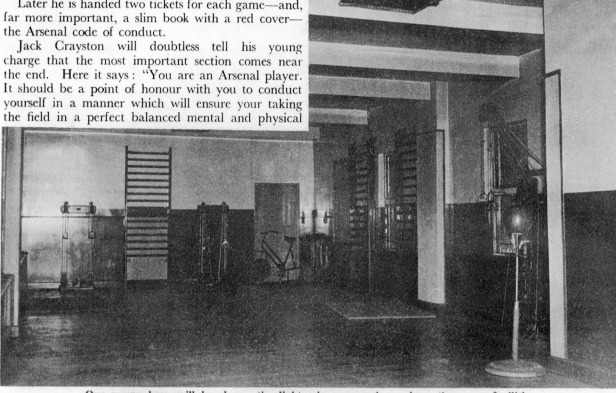

Our young hero will be shown the light, airy gymnasium where there are facilities for keeping fit when bad weather makes training outdoors impossible.

The Arsenal player can expect more than his share of hero-worship. Here is Joe Wade obliging some of his schoolboy fans.

▲ 1953–54 Gift Book

. . . FILING CABINET . .

In the dressing-room, even the floors are warmed so that players can pad about in comfort in their bare feet as they prepare for a plunge in the luxurious baths (below).

· · YOU MAY JOIN ARSENAL · · ·

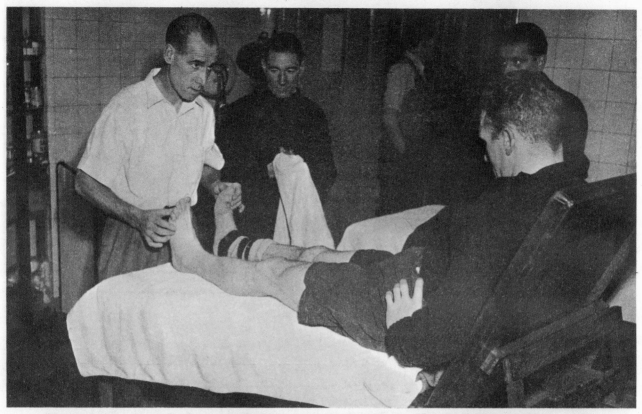

The newcomer will see the famous medical treatment rooms. Above, Alex Forbes is receiving attention while Jimmy Logie, another Scot, looks on. Below, those infra-red lamps do wonderful work in helping to cure aches and pains.

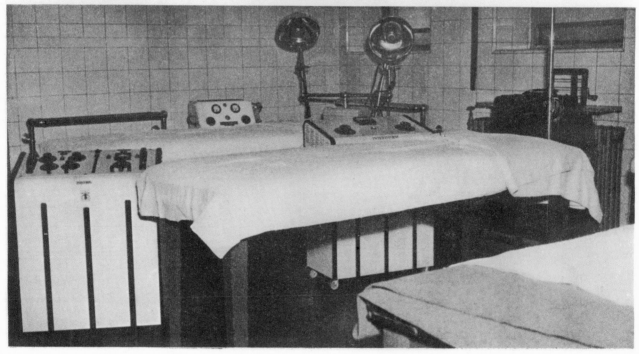

▲ 1953–54 Gift Book

. . . LIVE IN A SOCCER PALACE . . .

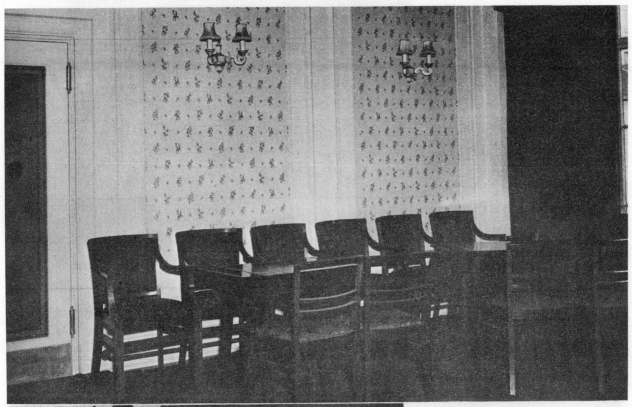

One of the "posh" lounges where guests at Arsenal games are entertained.

Even sunlight is at Arsenal's disposal! This "sunshine" lamp (left) helps to tone up the players during the long months of a London winter.

... SEE THE WORLD, & ENJOY LIFE

And during the close season Arsenal sometimes tour abroad. These pictures were taken on their visit to South America—they speak for themselves. Alex Forbes (left) is enjoying his soup, while, above, Jimmy Logie, complete with cigar, smile and victory sign, is obviously happy with his lot.

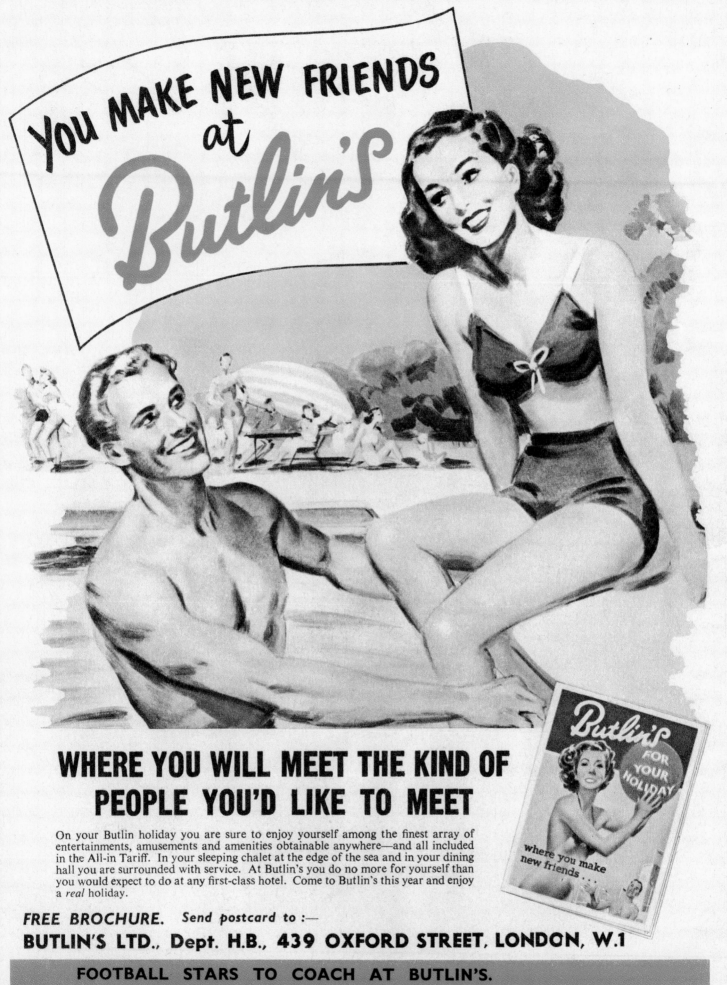

YOU MAKE NEW FRIENDS at *Butlin's*

WHERE YOU WILL MEET THE KIND OF PEOPLE YOU'D LIKE TO MEET

On your Butlin holiday you are sure to enjoy yourself among the finest array of entertainments, amusements and amenities obtainable anywhere—and all included in the All-in Tariff. In your sleeping chalet at the edge of the sea and in your dining hall you are surrounded with service. At Butlin's you do no more for yourself than you would expect to do at any first-class hotel. Come to Butlin's this year and enjoy a *real* holiday.

Butlin's FOR YOUR HOLIDAY

where you make new friends . . .

FREE BROCHURE. *Send postcard to :—*
BUTLIN'S LTD., Dept. H.B., 439 OXFORD STREET, LONDON, W.1

FOOTBALL STARS TO COACH AT BUTLIN'S.

First-class Soccer players will act as resident coaches at every Butlin Holiday Camp during the 1953 summer season, giving free tuition, available to all Campers. They'll be talent spotting, too, so here's your chance to bring your skill to the notice of the experts.

AR
MO

1 Charle
left) with
seeing tou
the backg
Cathedral

2 Action
decorate t
Dynamo S
teries of

3 Jimmy
holds a bo
way he wil

4 Mosco
That's Lo
(No. 3) a
pe

NAL
OW

(second from
nal on a sight-
Red Square. In
is St. Basil's
he right The
n.

of sportsmen
e of the Moscow
Note the bat-
s on the roof.

rsenal skipper,
d indicates the
er winning the

o on the attack.
), while Wade
es (right) are
action.

... FOR YOUR ALBUM

JIM BLOOMFIELD
Arsenal

RALPH GUTHRIE
Arsenal

ARTHUR MILTON
Arsenal

◀◀ December 1954

▲ Selected from 1954–55

ARSENAL

Standing—Goring, Bowen, Kelsey, Barnes, Wills, Forbes. Kneeling—Tapscott, Logie, Lawton, Lishman, Roper.

▲ December 1954

▲ October 1952

THEY MADE ME A GOALKEEPER –
because I was smallest!

By
JACK KELSEY
Arsenal and Wales

I 'VE always been a goalkeeper. Only once, in fact, have I ever played in any other position.

It was in a match for Winch Wen, the Swansea and District League club for whom I played in my amateur days. I turned out at centre-forward, but there was a special reason.

For a spell I had been keeping goal for the club, but was due to enter the Army. In order to give my successor a chance to find his feet, I was moved up into the attack.

No, I didn't impress everyone with a dazzling display of leadership. I did nothing of note. To tell the truth, I felt like a fish out of water. If anything, the experience convinced me that my proper place was between the posts. I have never since had any cause to change my mind about that.

When our club committee had suggested that I play at centre-forward, I readily agreed. Here, I thought, is a chance to try out some good, old-fashioned shoulder-charging on the opposing goalkeeper.

▲ 1954–55 Gift Book

Coming from a goalkeeper, that might strike an odd note. But I mean what I say.

Although I've taken a few knocks myself, I think forwards should make full use of the shoulder charge when the goalkeeper is in possession of the ball, providing, of course, that it is employed fairly and squarely.

After all, a goalkeeper should be capable of standing up to a firm, legitimate charge.

I did not choose goalkeeping in the first place . . . it was thrust upon me.

When I was very young, I played with older boys at our home village of Winch Wen, which is close to Llansamlet, just outside Swansea.

As I was younger and smaller than the others, it was decided that it would be dangerous for me to play out in the field.

So I was given the goalkeeping position, and have stuck to it ever since.

My career in organised schools football was remarkably brief. After I had played four games as goalkeeper for the junior team at the local Cwm School, the war broke out and put a stop to the competition. This was a great blow, and for two years I played no football at all.

Looking back, I'm sure that period of two years was not entirely wasted. Llansamlet is only three and a half miles from Swansea, and I was able to see Swansea Town in action at the Vetch Field.

Even at that time I was obsessed with the idea of becoming a professional footballer, although I felt I had little chance.

I watched the style and methods of the goalkeepers at the Vetch Field, trying as much as I could to learn something from them.

I remember Swansea playing a guest goalkeeper from Southampton named Len Stansbridge. Before the kick-off, he would mark a line in the turf with his foot, at right-angles to the six-yards line.

Watching from the terraces, I hadn't the faintest notion what he was doing, but I now know that he was making a landmark that would give him his bearings in relation to the goalposts.

This can be a tremendous help to a goalkeeper, and nowadays I do it myself as a safeguard against " losing " the location of my goalposts when advancing to meet an on-coming attack.

My experience of football in the Army was even briefer than my spell in the Cwm School team. I joined the Royal Engineers, and was sent to Wrexham.

My record with the Winch Wen team meant absolutely nothing in North Wales and I couldn't even get a game during recreational sessions.

I was dying to play football again, but for months I never had a kick at a ball. My first chance came while I was watching a game. One of the goalkeepers was a sergeant who had to go back on duty at half-time, and as I was on the spot, I took his place.

I think we held a 3—1 lead when I came on. Anyway, I let three in, and we lost 4—3. Don't blame me for the defeat. I played in full uniform, including big Army boots. The only thing missing was my kit-bag !

To that half of a match I can add only one other game of football during my Army days. And what a game it was !

My side lost 6—5, and each of our eleven players scored a goal. Our five forwards notched one each, and all their goals were touched in by *our* players. My own contribution was a mistimed punch.

You don't believe it ? Well, I know it sounds fantastic, but if any of my old sapper friends who were on the spot on that Sunday morning at Farnborough, in Hampshire, chance to read this, they at least will know my words are true.

By the way, Cliff Holton, who is now my team-mate

" It's *my* ball," Kelsey seems to be saying as he clutches it—safe from the feet of Tottenham's Sonny Walters.

with Arsenal, was in the camp team at Farnborough when I was there, but at that time we were unknown to each other.

When I left the Army, I returned to the Winch Wen team, and I had had a season and a half with them when the golden opportunity to step into big football came my way.

How close I came to missing it ! If my mother had had her way, I would never have played in the game that was to change the whole course of my life.

She had quite a good reason. My cousin was giving a twenty-first birthday party, and Mother felt I should take a day off from football in order to be on time for the celebrations.

I had no wish to disturb family harmony, but to miss playing in what happened to be the last match of the season was asking too much of any enthusiastic young footballer.

I insisted on playing, and by the time I rejoined the family at my cousin's party in the evening, I was glad I had.

We were among the lowly teams of the Swansea and District League, but our opponents that day, a team called the Ivorites, were at the top. We beat them 1—0, and I had one of those lucky days when everything comes off.

My biggest stroke of luck was that two penalty kicks were awarded against my side.

You see, I managed to stop both shots, and it happened that the opposing right-half, who had taken the spot-kicks, had been on Arsenal's books in pre-war days.

When the match ended he suggested putting me in touch with Arsenal, but the referee, who appeared to have some contact with Bolton Wanderers, seemed

And sometimes you end up by standing on your head.

That Brazilian forward (in the game against Portuguesa) looks rather disappointed that Kelsey reached the ball first.

▲ 1954–55 Gift Book

to think it would be better if a recommendation reached the Lancashire club.

The whole thing sounded so ridiculous to me that I refused to treat their suggestions seriously. Then the two of them argued for the right to sit next to me on the homeward bus!

The Arsenal man won, and during the journey he convinced me that he meant what he said.

That's how Arsenal first heard of me. Sounds like a fairy-tale, doesn't it?

Events moved rapidly from that stage. Before season 1949-50 opened, Arsenal suggested that I should have a run-out with Llanelly.

This arrangement meant that Arsenal's representative would be able to watch me perform in a higher standard of football than the local league.

It was a private trial at Llanelly. Unfortunately, I had very little to do, and I remember how disappointed I felt when I sat down in the dressing-room after the game, convinced that my opportunity had gone.

How little I knew of Arsenal! Their methods are much more thorough than that.

A week later I was instructed to report to Llanelly once more. This time I was given the job of guarding the reserve net against Llanelly's first team in a public trial.

There was nothing idle about that afternoon. Llanelly's senior attack was, of course, the strongest I had ever faced. Happily, I came through the test satisfactorily, and, apparently, a favourable report reached Highbury.

Next move was an invitation, almost immediately, for me to play in a private Wednesday trial at Highbury. I travelled to London and turned out in a side composed mainly of Arsenal's " A " team players.

The centre-half on my side that day was Len Wills, who is now Arsenal's right-back, and one of my closest friends.

Once again I had an easy match, but when it was over I was told the wonderful news that Arsenal were willing to sign me.

Cliff Holton and I were in the same camp team but we were then unknown to each other.

I WENT home, gave a week's notice to the firm in Llansamlet, where I had been working as a painter-rigger, and then returned to Highbury to commence my great adventure as an Arsenal footballer.

Words can scarcely describe the thrill of my early days at Highbury. Those two trials with Llanelly bridged my leap from Winch Wen to Arsenal. What a jump!

At the end of one season I was carrying my own kit to matches in a bag and suffering all the gladly-imposed discomforts that are inseparable from junior football. . . At the beginning of the next, I had a place in the luxurious dressing-room of the most famous club in the world of football.

Like all players, I have, of course, had my ups-and-downs since turning professional. I haven't the space to touch upon them now, but I've just enough left to tell you about my most profitable save.

We were beating Newcastle United 2—1, and only about two minutes were left to play.

Bobby Mitchell, Newcastle's outside-left, burst through and hit one of his specials. The ball flashed towards the top left-hand corner of the net, but somehow or other I managed to reach it with my finger-tips and push it round for a corner.

The following week I received from a spectator a letter enclosing a five-pound note in recognition of what he described as the " finest save he had ever seen."

I don't suppose I shall ever make a more " noteworthy " save than that!

First I met England's star, then the Russians . . .

MY Arsenal pals who have more Soccer service in years than I have in months, have often told me that the game a player never forgets is his first League match.

I fully endorse that now, especially as in my case the first League problem that I, as a centre-half, had to deal with was a fellow in a No. 9 shirt named Nat Lofthouse !

My second senior outing was against a Russian side in a match that had been lifted from the Sports Page to the Front Page—with the knowledge that millions were looking on through TV.

It all added up to quite an opening for a teenage Scot.

That was some week for me, last November. It began with a message to report to Mr. Whittaker's office on the Wednesday before our game with Bolton, at Burnden Park.

"The Boss" told me I would be playing, also that I was being given early notice to get used to the idea and so stave off last-minute nerves.

But only when he wished me luck did the news really sink in.

★

Nervous? I took it all very calmly—on Wednesday. On Thursday, thinking about the coming ordeal, I hardly ate anything! But by Saturday I felt quite composed.

Nat Lofthouse was a great sport and I thoroughly enjoyed our first meeting. We got a much needed point in a 2—2 draw.

Nat didn't score and it was this as much as anything, that brought me to the end of the match very much relieved.

I don't claim to be without nerves and I suppose the thoughts of playing against Spartak three days later should have been enough to worry anybody.

But I kidded myself into thinking that it was just another game, despite the trimmings that were being woven round it.

Honestly, I couldn't get over-excited about the match. I suppose that is why I went out to have what I feel is my best game so far.

★

We Arsenal players tried all we knew to wipe out the memory of that 5—0 beating by Moscow Dynamo, a month earlier. Maybe if we had got that second half penalty for a foul on Arthur Milton, our right-winger, we would have made it a draw.

But though we went down 2—1 we all knew that we had done something to atone partially, at least, for the Moscow beating.

For Arsenal were a grand team that night. In all modesty we can claim to have blown up the theories that Spartak were world-beaters—Wolves later confirmed the point.

That first week of mine is, naturally, the high spot in a modest career that has yet to stretch to a full season. But there was another week when it seemed that things might work out in rather hectic fashion for me.

Looking back now I am rather fright-

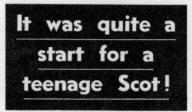

It was quite a start for a teenage Scot !

ened at the thought that my first big game might have been at Wembley in the Cup Final. Here are the facts. . . .

Three years ago Arsenal, due to meet Newcastle, at Wembley, had the unluckiest bunch of injuries a club could have. Jimmy Logie and Doug Lishman were hospital cases and Ray Daniel, our centre-half, had a broken wrist in plaster and was very doubtful.

★

I was the reserve centre-half, but right-half Arthur Shaw—with much more experience—was given a game at centre-half in case he had to take Ray's place. And Arthur also broke an arm.

I had read in some newspapers that Arsenal might have to call on a young unknown for the Final. His name was Jim Fotheringham, and those reports made me very nervous.

I doubt if I was seriously considered at the time, but Arthur's injury made the situation even more desperate.

Perhaps I solved it. That Saturday before the Final I fell against our goal-post in trying to head away a corner.

★

I caught the bottom of my spine and my legs became paralysed. They had to carry me off and I spent the next week in hospital.

But for my football I would have followed father into his trade as an engineer.

My father came to Corby, Northants— "Little Scotland," they call it—when I was 18 months old. Many people are surprised at my Scottish accent when I tell them I have been in England so long—but Corby and thousands of exiled Scots explains that.

Like most Scots kids it was Rangers for me in the early days—even at some 400 miles range.

Too busy playing, I saw little senior football as a youngster. But in Scotland

on holidays I usually managed to see a game or two there, and big Frank Brennan was my favourite. He was then playing for Airdrie.

My school games were played in the Samuel Lloyd School side, I was a left-back then. Then came a move on to Corby Technical College and a change to centre-half.

I also represented Northampton Youth and was thrilled at the news that Sunderland and Leicester scouts were watching me.

But before then came a chance for me, a Scot, to play for England Schoolboys. I was picked for the South team to meet the North in a trial at Oxford.

★

A few days before the game I went down with 'flu, but scared that I would miss my chance, I pretended to be better on the day. I made a real hash of things and bang went a cap.

Strange, something like that almost happened to me on another occasion when I had my heart set on a game. I got the chance to play for the Army against Scotland, at Hampden Park, during my service days.

It was a wonderful thrill—until a troublesome boil on the face almost closed my left eye. I had daily penicillin injections, but it was nowhere near right on the day and again I had to pretend that I was much better than I really was.

But who wouldn't have done the same in my place? We lost 2—1, but I had the privilege and pleasure of meeting fellows like George Young, Tommy Ring and Bobby Johnstone that afternoon.

★

My father, to my surprise, would not hear of trials at either Sunderland or Leicester for me. Much later I found out that he had had his eyes and his hopes on a London club for me.

An Arsenal scout was the first to enter our sitting room, and, in 1949, I was off to Highbury.

So keen was I to make good that I spent a fortnight's holiday there in order to be really fit for my test. I was determined not to let my father or myself down.

My first game was against Leyton Orient in the London Mid-Week League. I was then 16.

Now, at 6ft. 3¾in., they tell me I'm the tallest player in the game. Well, it's handy, to say the least, when the ball is in the air.

I have had the best of coaching from great players and great colleagues like Alf Field and Leslie Compton—and Tommy Lawton has been long-suffering and a model of patience in teaching me how best to head a ball.

And Arsenal? Even to a football rookie like me it is so obviously the best club in the world !

▲ July 1955

DEREK TAPSCOTT says

They didn't tell me it was Arsenal!

MY football career started with a mystery journey. Let me explain.

One evening, after I had finished my day's work on the maintenance staff of the local council at Barry, South Wales, I returned home to find Mr. Bill Jones, who was then manager of Barry Town, having a chat with my mother over a cup of tea.

I was a Barry player at the time, but was quite unprepared for the news that followed.

"Your ambition is coming true," said Mr. Jones. "I'm not giving any names away, but I'm taking you to London tomorrow for an interview with a First Division club."

I tried to wheedle the name of the club out of him, but Mr. Jones, who is now manager of Worcester City, would not budge.

What a field of conjecture his words opened up. The fact that we were bound for London did not necessarily imply that we would be calling on a London club.

It could mean, I reasoned, that a Midland or Northern club had arranged a meeting in London.

I was in the seventh heaven of delight, but Mr. Jones, aided and abetted by Mr. John Bailey, the Barry director, preserved the air of secrecy over our precise destination during the train journey from Cardiff to London.

My mind drifted over the entire network of the First Division without daring to dwell on any particular club. I knew I might be in for a disappointment if I formed the idea that I had attracted the attention of one of the more famous clubs.

All I knew for certain was that it was not Cardiff . . . our departure from Cardiff General Station had told me that!

At Paddington Station the truth came out. We descended to the Underground railway, and as Mr. Jones approached the booking office I kept close to his side.

"Arsenal Station," I heard him say to the booking clerk, and with a benevolent smile he turned to watch the effect of those magic words upon me.

So that was it! Arsenal, of all clubs, were interested in me. It was news worth waiting for, and I sensed that Mr. Jones felt relief that our destination was no longer secret.

If he meant to give me a wonderful surprise, he certainly succeeded. In quick time we were at Arsenal

Stadium, where another surprise awaited me. Needless to say, I was nervous. I had never seen anything as lavish as Arsenal's ground, and I felt very small and insignificant as I mounted the stairs to the office of Mr. Tom Whittaker, Arsenal's secretary-manager.

His friendly manner helped to put me at ease, however, and I was encouraged to hear his remark that I was bigger than he had expected.

I was told that Arsenal would watch me play for Barry against Headington United, but after I had been shown around the Highbury ground—it was worth travelling from South Wales for that experience alone—I was recalled to Mr. Whittaker's office, and told that the plan had been changed. Arsenal were willing to sign me on the spot!

That set the seal on an unforgettable day and as I left Mr. Whittaker's office that evening Bill Dickson passed me on his way in. It's funny how incidents like that stick in the mind. Bill was then a Chelsea player, and I think he signed for Arsenal on the following day.

I shall never forget the thrill of those early days at Arsenal Stadium. Before playing in a match of any kind, I was introduced to all the players and given an opportunity to adjust myself to the Arsenal atmosphere.

Then came my first game, at inside-left, in the reserve side on Queen's Park Rangers' ground.

That match was not only important to me as my first in Arsenal's colours, it was also the occasion of an interesting reunion.

When I was serving in the Royal Engineers at Aldershot there was a chap in my barrack-room named Jim Fotheringham.

Now I was the N.C.O. in charge of that barrack-room, and big Jim was under my orders. But that didn't stop me envying him. Jim was an Arsenal player, and the only professional footballer in our unit.

Yes, it's the same Jim Fotheringham who is now Arsenal's centre-half. And when I reported with Arsenal for that first game on the Rangers' ground, there was my old barrack-room friend, who was still in the Army at that time.

What a laugh we had at meeting under such vastly different circumstances.

We won the game 2—1 and I was kept in Arsenal's reserve team for the next match. We played at Brighton and in that game my progress came to a swift halt. I injured a shoulder, and was out of action for five weeks.

That injury dealt me a disappointing blow, but I recall an earlier injury that played a big part in helping me up the Soccer ladder.

After I left school I joined Barry West End, one of the local amateur clubs. We had a good team, and won a number of trophies.

One Saturday I injured my knee, and in order to get proper treatment I called on Mr. Albert Gardner, who was then trainer to the Barry Town club.

While attending to my injured knee, he asked me if I would sign amateur forms for Barry. I had supported the club since schooldays, and was glad to accept his offer. So an injured knee was the means of lifting me into the Barry Town fold.

Barry made it clear that I could carry on playing with the West End club when I was not required for one of their own teams, and everybody seemed to be happy about the arrangement.

I was then 17 and was recognised as a centre-forward. My weight was only 9st. and Barry decided that I was too small and frail for that position.

They switched me to outside-right and looking back I feel sure their decision was a wise one. I settled down on the wing and after joining the Army kept to the outside-right berth in service matches.

It was while I was playing in Army football at Aldershot that the Spurs began to display an interest in me. A scout had watched me a few times, but no definite approach had been made to me until one afternoon when our unit game was called off owing to snow.

I was in the dressing-room, somewhat depressed at the prospect of missing an afternoon's football, when I was told someone wanted to see me outside.

He was Tottenham's representative and until then I was unaware that I had been under observation. When

Training conference at Highbury. Left to right are Walley Barnes, trainer Billy Milne, Arthur Milton —now with Bristol City—and manager Tom Whittaker.

▲ 1955–56 Gift Book

SIGN HERE, PLEASE ! The schools are on holiday, the young fans of North London wait outside Highbury . . . and Derek Tapscott obliges.

he explained his identity, I was quite excited at the possibility of joining Spurs and readily agreed to play a trial.

Two days later I had a letter from Spurs, inviting me to play in their London Mid-Week League team against Fulham at Craven Cottage. We won the match 2—1 and I felt I had done reasonably well, especially as it was my first game in professional company.

After the match Tottenham told me they would get in touch with me later on. But I heard nothing more.

At the time it was a disappointment for me, but similar experiences have befallen many players. It's all part of football life, and if taken in the right spirit, serves to condition a player against the rebuffs that are inseparable from the game.

I've just space to tell you of my most memorable moment.

In April, 1954, I played my first League game for Arsenal, against Liverpool at Highbury. We won 3—0 and I managed to score two of the goals.

On the following Monday I received a telegram from the directors of Barry Town wishing me the best of luck and many more caps.

I couldn't understand a message like that and imagined there had been some confusion with my debut in Arsenal's League team. A day later, however, I was called into Mr. Whittaker's office after training and told the tremendous news that I had been nominated as one of the players to form the Welsh F.A. party travelling to Austria.

I then realised that my Barry friends had been first with the news and when I reached my lodgings I was handed a congratulatory telegram from Mother and Dad back home at Barry.

Then came the thrill of all thrills. On the radio at 6.25 that evening I heard the Welsh team announced, with yours truly at inside-right.

Reality had exceeded my wildest dream. I was to fly to Vienna to play for Wales against Austria. I'll leave you to guess how much that meant to a young Welshman, new to League football, who had never been abroad before, and had never previously travelled in an aircraft.

My Goodness!

Guinness with your meals
—that's quite a thing!

WHY IS IT THAT so many chaps enthuse about Guinness almost as if it were something new? Well, perhaps it *is* new to them, and they never realized before how delicious Guinness was.

But once you've enjoyed its rich, refreshing flavour you'll say to yourself, here at last is something really worth drinking. And it is, you know. Try a glass with your midday meal.

G.E.2362.M

▲ September 1954

Charles Buchan's
FOOTBALL
MONTHLY

1'6

Overseas Price 2/-
Forces Overseas 1/6

SEPTEMBER
1956

VIC GROVES
Arsenal

A cosy little corner . . .

. . . A corner in which Vic Groves, of Arsenal, feels a warm glow of pleasure as he stands beside the trophies he has won during his thrill-studded Soccer career. They are in his bedroom in his London home.

▲ 1956–57 Gift Book

Full of the joy of springing over Stan Charlton is Vic Groves. Both had just joined Arsenal when this picture was taken

Groves is a very modern - minded young man. That's why he is keen to experiment with a new cut - away boot (top). It gives more speed than the old pattern.

Have your feet ever felt as heavy as lead? Imagine how Groves feels, then, as he strengthens his muscles with this weight on his right foot.

Nothing to do with the picture on the left. This is Groves being treated for a " field " injury by Billy Milne.

DANNY CLAPTON
Arsenal

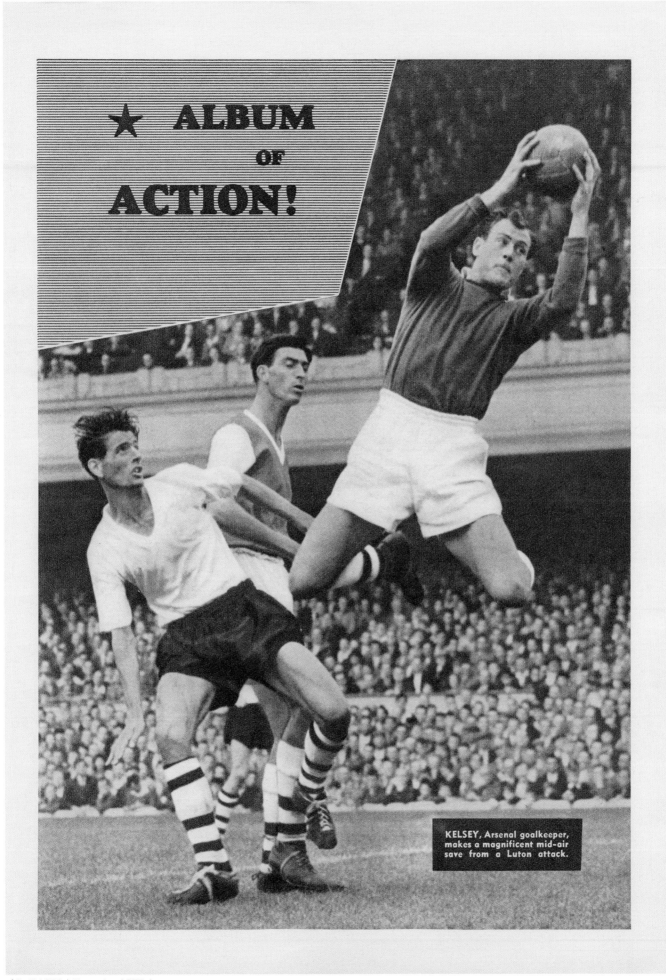

★ ALBUM OF ACTION!

KELSEY, Arsenal goalkeeper, makes a magnificent mid-air save from a Luton attack.

THE TRUTH

Dodgin wards off Tom Finney as Kelsey dives to push the ball away.

Again, Dodgin is where the danger is. This time he is helping Kelsey check a raid by Manchester United's Tommy Taylor.

by
BILL DODGIN
Arsenal

I'VE heard it said that adversity is the test of ability. In my experience, I feel that to be so, for it acts as an incentive—an extra challenge to stiffen resolve and determination.

I'm not suggesting that Dame Fortune has dealt me any severe blows, but after playing regularly in Arsenal's League team in season 1953-54, I lost my place and had only three or four senior matches in the next eighteen months.

It is true I had lost form, but that was a long period of obscurity after holding such a regular place in the senior team. **Looking back, however, I know it did me a world of good.**

It conditioned me against the rebuffs that seem to lurk around the corner in football, and filled me with new determination.

Although I missed only three League matches in 1953-54, that was the season in which I asked the late Tom Whittaker to drop me !

We had a shocking start to that season. After our first seven matches we were without a win, had only two points to our credit, and were bottom of the League.

Our next game was at Sunderland and the result did nothing to brighten the atmosphere at Arsenal Stadium. We lost 7-1.

On the Tuesday we were due to visit Chelsea, who had won at Highbury the previous week.

▲ May 1957

'BEHIND MY MOVE TO THE WORLD'S GREATEST CLUB'

Before that Chelsea game I went to Mr. Whittaker and asked to be dropped. I thought I was doing the right thing—that I would be making things easier for him.

I left his office quicker than I entered it. He told me very firmly that if there was any dropping to be done, he would do it.

So I stayed in the team, and the tide turned that very day.

We beat Chelsea 2-0, and took seven points from the next four games. When the season ended, we were twelfth—a good recovery after that bad start.

I signed for Arsenal in October, 1949. My father had always lavished great praise on Arsenal.

"The greatest club in the world," he always said. And, knowing his wide experience of the game, I knew they were no idle words.

Now, of course, I have proof of how right he was.

Perhaps the thing that impressed me most when I became an Arsenal player was the standard of the training kit.

Everything is first-class, down to the smallest detail. I never felt more immaculate than when I donned Arsenal training kit for the first time.

Fulham gave me my chance as a professional.

I had always wanted to play in big football. When I was a small boy, my father was a half-back for Clapton (now Leyton) Orient, Bristol Rovers and Southampton.

When I left school I became an apprenticed draughtsman at an aircraft factory in Southampton. I suppose it could have provided me with a good job, but my heart was not in it.

Dad was managing Southampton at that time and I was playing as an amateur in the club's "A" team.

In the summer of 1949 he took over as team manager of Fulham and I was given a game in Fulham's "A" team against Tudor Rose, Chelsea's junior team, in an R.A.F. charity match.

Bobby Smith, now with Spurs, was playing centre-forward for Tudor Rose.

I didn't attach any great importance to that particular match. As it happened, however, everything came off for me, especially in the first half.

I played at left-back, and Frank Osborne, Fulham's general manager, wanted to sign me.

My father stayed neutral. He fore-saw the difficulties that could arise if I played under his management.

Anyway, I accepted Fulham's offer and became a professional with the club.

When I left Fulham for Arsenal, a lot was said about the treatment I had received from the Craven Cottage crowd, and that the barrackers influenced my departure.

This is quite wrong. I found the crowd and the players at Fulham to be all right, and I was happy enough at the Cottage.

Every fooballer comes in for criticism from time to time. He knows he can't please all the people always.

It's nice to know the crowd is with you, but if at times they're not, you've got to put up with it. I certainly don't let it worry me.

The truth is that I moved to Arsenal simply because they wanted to sign me, and Fulham were prepared to part.

I think it eased things for Dad. We never had any difficulty at Fulham, but as long as I was a player under his team management, I suppose there was always the possibility of an embarrassing situation arising for him.

As the son of a League footballer, it is obvious that I got a lot of good advice at a young age.

Dad was always urging me to apply thought to my game. That is good counsel, but in fact, I have at times found myself applying too much thought to my football.

Don Revie, the Sunderland inside-right, is a first-class example of the thinking player.

Don is not alone. Of the centre-forwards I have faced, Tom Finney (Preston), Tommy Taylor (Manchester United), Ronnie Allen (West Bromwich) and Bill Holden, the former Burnley player, who is now with Stockport, are four who spring to mind as thoughtful and intelligent players.

Concentration cannot be relaxed, even momentarily, against that type. He engages his opponent in a battle of wits in addition to testing his football skill.

Just to make sure the ball is cleared, three Arsenal defenders go for it — including, of course, Dodgin.

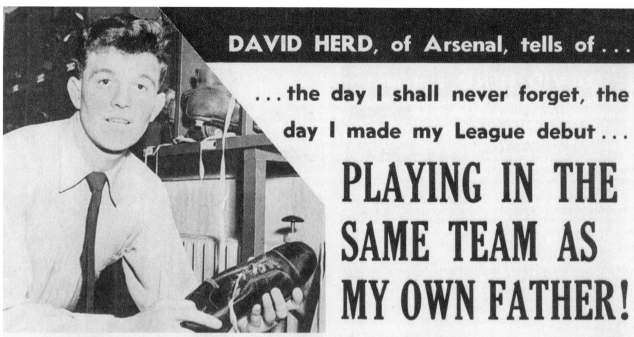

...the day I shall never forget, the day I made my League debut...

PLAYING IN THE SAME TEAM AS MY OWN FATHER!

FOOTBALL'S a thrilling, colourful business. I became a professional at seventeen, and have had my share of excitement. One occasion stands out in my Soccer life, however, and whatever my fortunes may be in the future, I'm sure it will never lose its special place in my memory.

I refer to my League début with Stockport County in May, 1951. A début is a big enough occasion for any player, but mine was memorable for an extra reason—I was playing in the same forward line as my father, who was nearing the end of a distinguished career. He was the Alec Herd who played at inside-forward for Hamilton Academicals and Manchester City.

Naturally, I was brought up in a football atmosphere, and always wanted to become a professional myself. But never in my most fanciful moments did the thought occur to me that I might play in the same team as my father in League football.

It was the last League game of the season, and we were at home to Hartlepools United. In all, it was quite a week for me.

Only a few days after I had signed professional forms, I was given my first game in Stockport's Cheshire League team in an evening match at Stalybridge. I scored a goal, and to my surprise and joy was promoted to the first team for the following Saturday's match by Andy Beattie, our manager.

Two other 17-year-olds—left-winger Keith Goalen and right-winger Brian Brennan—were also in that Stockport team.

I was on the programme at inside-right, but at the kick-off

I filled the inside-left position. The reason? In my excitement, I took up the wrong position!

Dad noticed it, but decided to leave me alone. He took the inside-right position himself and I switched with him to take my intended place after half-time.

His presence on the field that day—we won the match 2-0—was of tremendous help to me. The home truths I heard at half-time were invaluable!

Dad's prime was spent with Manchester City, and although I was born at Hamilton, I was brought up at Moss Side, Manchester.

Needless to say, I had some first-class instruction from an early age—with a ball in the back garden. We lived in Clinton Avenue, and a few doors away lived Dennis Viollet, now the star inside-left of Manchester United. Dennis and I were great pals. We spent hours kicking about together on a pitch at Fallowfield.

I attended Princess Road School, Moss Side, and was the envy of all the boys with football in their blood. The reason was that I trained with the Manchester City players while still at school.

Dad used to take me along to the ground. Imagine what a thrill it was for me to find myself practising alongside famous players like Jack Bray and Sam Barkas.

I remember the first day I trained with the City players at Maine Road. I went through the same programme as the pros and was so exhausted at the finish I felt really ill!

Dad was transferred to Stockport in 1948. We moved there

(Continued on next page)

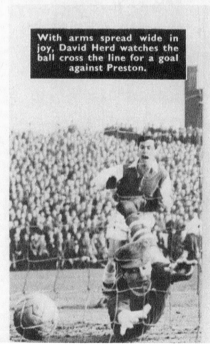

With arms spread wide in joy, David Herd watches the ball cross the line for a goal against Preston.

▲ July 1957

DAVID HERD continued

and I signed as an amateur for the club at 15. Then came a spell in the club's junior team. With me in that side was George Ashfield, the full-back who is now with Aston Villa.

It was my father who first broke the news that Arsenal were interested in me. I was then nearing the end of my R.A.F. service.

I came home on leave, and he asked me how I would like to join Arsenal. I could hardly believe his words to be true. Like any other ambitious young footballer, I was overjoyed at the chance.

The late Tom Whittaker, then Arsenal's manager, watched me in a trial match at Stockport. I was unaware of his presence, which was just as well. I might have been over-anxious had I known. As it was, everything went well, and I managed to score three goals. I suppose that went a long way towards guiding my steps to Highbury.

The transfer deal went through within a few hours of my demob from the R.A.F. I travelled home from my station at Catterick, in Yorkshire, changed into civvies and then dashed to a Manchester hotel, where Mr. Whittaker was waiting for me.

Twice only had I seen Arsenal play. I saw Newcastle beat them in the 1952 Cup Final and I was on Manchester City's ground the day Frank Swift was due to play his last game as City's goalkeeper.

Arsenal beat City 3-0 that day. As it happened, Frank came out of his retirement to play a few more games the following season.

I may not have seen much of Arsenal before joining them, but I needed no telling that I had joined one of the finest clubs in football. And the first visit to the dressing-rooms at Arsenal Stadium left me truly amazed. **I had never seen anything so imposing on any Soccer ground.**

Joining Arsenal has enabled me to travel abroad under first-class conditions. I had never been abroad until I was taken to Moscow as reserve to the team that played the Dynamo. What a maiden trip !

Dave carries out some light training with the skipping rope in the gym at Highbury.

We were well beaten, but it was an unforgettable experience. Nothing impressed me more than the fabulous collection of jewels in the Kremlin. There were treasures from all over Russia—their worth must be incalculable.

I have since been to Switzerland, France and Germany with Arsenal. There's always plenty of fun on overseas tours, and I'm sure they do a lot to cement team spirit.

There are practical jokers in every club, but as long as their plots don't go too far, no harm is done. I remember falling—with other players—for a hoax in Zurich. We were told that a certain film was showing in the town, and spent hours wandering about looking for the cinema.

It was pouring with rain, and we were soaked by the time we gave up and returned to our hotel. We then discovered we were the victims of a joke. The film was not showing at all.

It sharpens your wits for the next time !

JUBILATION

G-O-A-L! You could hear the shout echoing round the Valley as Derek Tapscott rejoiced over Arsenal's third score against Charlton.

▲ 1957–58 Gift Book

NOVEMBER 1957

Overseas Price 2/-
Forces Overseas 1/6

1/6

Charles Buchan's
FOOTBALL
MONTHLY

JOE HAVERTY
Arsenal and
Republic of Ireland

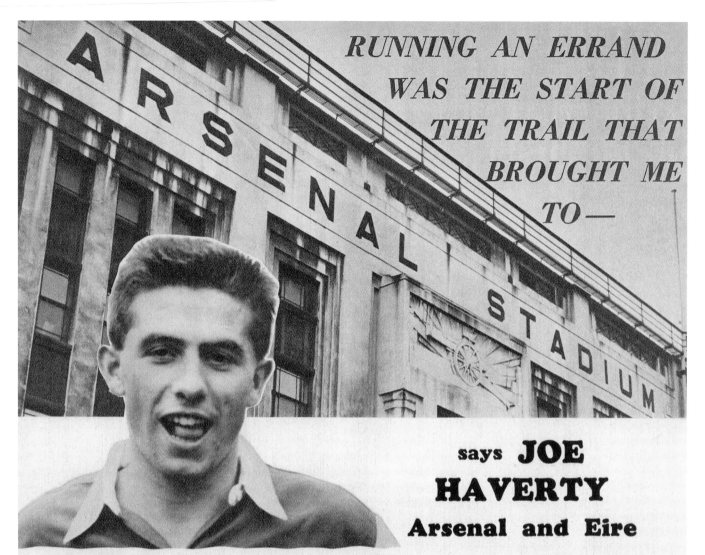

says **JOE**
HAVERTY
Arsenal and Eire

IT was quite by accident that I joined my first Soccer club. I lived in the Whitehall district of Dublin, and attended the Marino School. The school game was Gaelic football, and Soccer was a secondary recreation which we had to organise among ourselves in our spare time.

In my home district, a Soccer team was run by the Holy Child Boys' Club. The idea of joining it never occurred to me, but one day a boy at the Marino School asked if I would call on the club and arrange for him to join.

I agreed, and duly called on an official of the club. He accepted my school-friend as a member—and also persuaded me to join !

So an errand on a friend's behalf produced an unexpected result for me.

I was then only twelve, but even at that time I was an outside-left. My brother Paddy had played outside-left for Dublin Bohemians.

This, and the fact that I was small, may have influenced my choice of position. Also, my left foot was pretty reliable.

I won't say too much about the strength of my right at that time, but it has improved a lot since those days. Much of the credit goes to Alf Fields, Arsenal's coach and former centre-half.

Alf's patience and coaching skill were of tremendous help to me in my early days at Highbury.

After one year with the boys' club, I joined Home Farm. I stayed there for three seasons, and then came my chance with St. Patrick's Athletic.

I signed as an amateur and played for their minor team.

While a Home Farm player I was picked as reserve for the Eire Boys' team against Wales at Newport.

I had played in a scratch team against the chosen Eire side on the Home Farm ground, in a work-out which gave the Eire team a chance to play together before the big match.

The Eire outside-left was injured, and I was taken as reserve in case he was unable to play.

I was unlucky ! The selected left-winger was declared O.K., so I had to be satisfied with a place on the touch-line.

Now I have a memento of that occasion—we were all presented with a green neck-tie.

I shall always remember my League début for St. Patrick's.

I came home from the pictures one night and went straight to bed. I was asleep when my father opened the front door to an official of the St. Patrick's club.

They needed me for a City Cup match at Dundalk the following day. I was aroused and told the good

▲ 1957–58 Gift Book

news—the excitement did not help me to get off to sleep again quickly.

We beat Dundalk 1-0, and it was my centre that was handled by a home defender in the penalty area. That spot-kick won us the game.

I remember another game against Dundalk, on the Shamrock Rovers' ground at Milltown—our ground at St. Patrick's was not up to League standard at that time, so we used Rovers' ground for home matches.

We won this game 7-1. My wing partner was Alex Stevenson, the famous old Irish international of Glasgow Rangers and Everton. It was an honour and an education to play alongside him.

Luck plays a big part in football, and it was lucky for me that David Jack, famous old Arsenal inside-right, was managing Shelbourne at the time I was playing for St. Patrick's.

Mr. Jack was still in touch with Arsenal and he came and asked me if I would like to go to Highbury.

I had been approached by Ipswich Town shortly before then, but I had turned their offer down.

The glamorous prospect of joining Arsenal took my breath away. Of course, I agreed.

What an experience it was to report at Highbury! I was in another world. I never knew a football ground could be like Arsenal Stadium.

The luxury of the dressing-rooms and the impressive lay-out of the rest of the ground told me at once that I had come to the finest place in football.

I had seen Arsenal play only once. That was at Dalymount Park, Dublin, when they came over for an exhibition game against a team representing the Bohemians.

That day I watched from the terraces, full of admiration for Arsenal's Archie Macaulay, whose display was the talk of Dublin for weeks.

My first match for Arsenal was in the Eastern Counties League at March. We won 2-0.

It was the first game of the season and so I could scarcely believe my luck when I was selected for Arsenal's League team for a match at Everton on the following Wednesday.

That was nearly as big a thrill as viewing Arsenal's ground as a new player for the first time.

We lost 1-0 at Everton, but I stayed in the team for the following Saturday's match at West Bromwich.

In all, I had six League matches that season. In the next campaign I had eight.

Although it is not long since I left Dublin for London, it has been an eventful time for me. My job at home was as an apprenticed wire-worker.

Compare that with playing for the Arsenal!

I've just enough space left to tell you of an amusing incident in Germany, although it didn't seem funny at the time.

I was in that country as a member of the Eire Youth team, and we were staying in a village.

We were making our way to a shop where soft drinks were on sale and we all agreed that the last man in the shop should pay.

One player was so keen to avoid paying that he ran through what he thought was an open door.

It happened to be a full-length glass window, and splinters flew everywhere!

Fortunately, he was not hurt, but we all had to whip round to pay the owner for the damage.

ARSENAL : Standing—Wills, Charlton, Kelsey, Dodgin, Evans. Sitting—Bowen, Clapton, Tapscott, Holton, Bloomfield, Haverty.

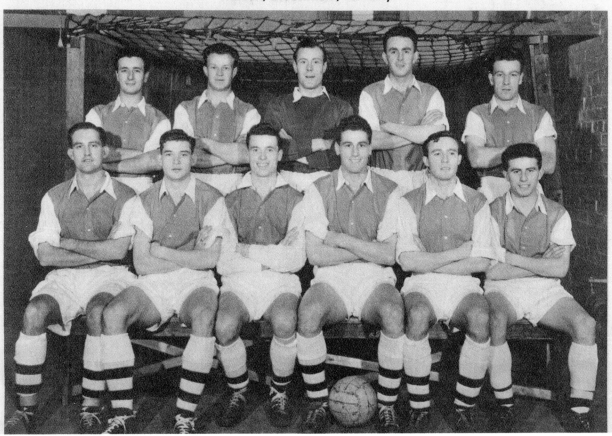

One day I was on my way to Griffin Park to play for Brentford when I saw a newspaper placard . . .

DAILY NEWS

ARSENAL WANT BLOOMFIELD

that was how I learned of

A DREAM WHICH HAS COME TRUE

by

JIMMY BLOOMFIELD
Arsenal

I STOOD on the terraces beneath the big clock on Arsenal's ground. England were playing Switzerland, and it was my first visit to Highbury.

That was in December, 1948. If anyone had then suggested that the famous pitch would one day be my home ground, I should have thought him out of his mind!

That international match stands out clearly in my memory. England won 6—o. Jack Rowley, the present Plymouth Argyle manager, who was then with Manchester United, was England's inside-right.

In the second half he scored one of the finest goals I have ever seen. He hit the ball from about forty yards with his left foot.

It was in the back of the net before the Swiss goalkeeper could move.

Only on one other occasion between that match and the day I signed for Arsenal, in the summer of 1954, was I at the Highbury ground.

That was a Christmas match between Arsenal and Blackpool. I was then a Brentford player, and George Bristow, who still plays at wing-half for them, came with me.

RON GREENWOOD . . . he was Brentford's centre-half.

Signing for Arsenal was a great thrill —a thing most young footballers dream about.

I knew nothing of Arsenal's interest in me until I read about it on a newspaper placard while on my way to Griffin Park to play for Brentford. When I arrived at the ground, Bill Dodgin, our manager, confirmed the exciting news.

There was no rush about the deal; I was not transferred until about six months later.

I had always wanted to be a professional footballer, and as a small boy, there was only one club for me—Queen's Park Rangers.

We lived in North Kensington, and all our family supported the Rangers. We had scrap-books devoted entirely to the club.

My main enjoyment was watching matches at the Loftus Road ground.

I even travelled to Derby with the boys from our street when Rangers were drawn against the County in the sixth round of the Cup in 1948.

They had drawn 1—1 at Shepherd's Bush, but Rangers were crushed 5—o at Derby. Reg Allen, Rangers' goalkeeper, was taken off, injured, but came back to play on the wing.

Remember Ted Hinton, the Irish international who kept goal for Millwall? Ted was then training our boys' club team in Kensington.

He gave me a letter of introduction to Dave Mangnall, who was then managing the Rangers. You can imagine what a thrill that was for me.

I went to the ground and was told that as I was so small, a couple of evenings training each week would do me a bit of good.

For eight months I went to train, but nothing came of it.

At St. Clement's School, North Kensington, I was a centre-forward. I certainly was small for that position. You get a lot of buffeting in the centre, so I switched to inside-forward.

I played for the Kensington Boys team, but I gained more honours at cricket than at football in my schooldays. I played for the Kensington and North-West London schools cricket teams. My first love was football, however.

I was only 16 when I was introduced to Hayes, the Athenian League club. I got a place in the first team, and began to feel I was getting somewhere.

Spurs made me an offer, but our coach at Hayes was George Wilkins, the old Brentford inside-forward. I also knew Ron Greenwood, then Brentford's centre-half, and I had good reason to believe that a place would be found for me at Griffin Park.

I signed amateur forms for Brentford before going into the Army.

Before my National Service was over I turned professional with Brentford and I had the luck to play for them when Tommy Lawton was with the club.

I owe a lot to Tommy. As Chelsea's centre-forward he had been my schoolboy idol. At Brentford he did a lot to knock the rough edges off my play.

(Continued on next page)

▲ January 1958

BLOOMFIELD
Continued from page 7

His criticism was always constructive, and he was always ready to give praise.

Tommy was, of course, player-manager to Brentford. When he left, Bill Dodgin took over. He also gave me a lot of help, and it was for this reason that I recommended my brother Billy to him.

Billy, like myself an inside-forward, was given a job on the Brentford ground staff. Now he is in his first full season as a professional.

I like to feel that I have helped Billy along the Soccer path. Although I am six years his senior, I used to spend a lot of time kicking a ball about with him. For hours we used to practise with a rubber ball at the top of our street.

It is an ambition of mine that one day—some way or other—we will find ourselves playing in the same team.

I believe a player can improve himself by watching as many matches as possible. In London we have plenty of opportunity of attending games on other grounds.

I watch each move closely, and visualise what I would do in the various situations which arise during the match.

I feel this is an excellent mental exercise. I encourage my brother to do the same thing.

In football you can never stop learning, and I reckon that if I apply thought to a situation I see as a spectator, my reaction is likely to be sharper if I find myself in a similar position when playing myself.

TOMMY LAWTON . . . was Bloomfield's schoolboy idol, and gave him plenty of sound advice.

I NEARLY TOOK FLIGHT BUT ARSENAL BROUGHT ME TO EARTH

Says
CLIFF HOLTON
of Arsenal

IT is funny how things work out. Only through a totally unexpected circumstance did I sign for Arsenal.

I decided to join the R.A.F. on an 8-year engagement. I was apprenticed as a tool-maker in an Oxford works at the time, but I wanted to become a flight mechanic. This meant cancelling my indentures.

I went through all the routine, including the medical examination, and was sent to Cardington. I signed everything, but was told I could not take the oath until I produced a copy of the indentures.

This was an unexpected snag. I was at Cardington for three days, but they sent me home pending the production of the missing documents.

What a good job they did so! While I was at home—expecting to return to Cardington within a few days—the secretary of Oxford City, the Isthmian League club, rang me with the exciting news that the *Arsenal were interested in me.*

I had been playing for Oxford City, and was spotted by Len Thompson, the Arsenal scout. My last match before reporting to Cardington was at Ilford, and he must have seen me in that game.

The chance to join Arsenal was too good to be missed. Although I had been keen to join the Air Force, I was greatly relieved that the formalities had not been completed. I was still free to change my mind.

Arsenal gave me a run-out at right-back against Cambridge University. I then signed as a professional, but was called up for Army service two months later.

I shall always remember my first game in Arsenal's Combination team. We were at home to Reading.

George Swindin, who now manages Peterborough, was in goal for us.

The first ball I had to deal with came my way after five minutes.

I went up to head it away, but George shouted "Right!". I left it to him, but his punch also connected with my head—and knocked me out!

Strange that my first match for Arsenal's reserves should have been against Reading. I was brought up in Oxford, and Reading was the nearest big club.

The first professional match I ever saw was on Reading's ground during the war. And oddly enough, Reading's visitors were Arsenal.

That was quite a day for me. My mother handed me a half-crown, and off I went with the main object of watching two players.

One was the celebrated Cliff Bastin, still playing for Arsenal at that time; the other was Matt Busby,

▲ 1958–59 Gift Book

Manchester United's famous manager, who was then playing as a guest for Reading.

Football came naturally enough to me from an early age. My father had played in the forward line of Oxford City, and had captained the team.

I'm told I was kicking a ball about when I was only eighteen months old. If you've a footballing father, it follows that you grow up with a ball at your feet. He was always throwing one to me from different angles.

I had just left school at fifteen when I was asked to play for Oxford City's reserves. I accepted the invitation, but kept my father in the dark.

I had a reason for that. He was on the club's committee, and I wanted to prove myself without any influence from him. He was delighted when he discovered I was playing for the club.

My first game for the Oxford City first team was against an Icelandic touring team which included Albert Gudmundsson, the inside-forward who afterwards joined Arsenal.

We won the game 3—1, and I scored one of the goals.

I played at inside-right, right-half and other positions before settling down at left-back.

Before joining the Oxford club, I had played for Marston Minors, the outstanding under-16 team in the county.

I was only twelve when I joined them. They needed an outside-left; I needed a game. So I claimed to be an outside-left. That seemed as good a way as any of getting into the team.

I was switched to centre-forward for Arsenal by the late Tom Whittaker. It was on Easter Saturday, 1950.

The first team were at Blackpool, and Tom rang through to Jack Crayston—now our manager, who was then in charge of the reserve team—and told him to play me at centre-forward against Fulham reserves.

Apparently we were hard pressed for a reserve centre-forward that day.

CLIFF BASTIN . . . the celebrated Arsenal winger whom Holton went specially to watch.

A strong wind was blowing, and I recall that Bill Dodgin, our present centre-half, was marking me for Fulham. We won 2—0. I scored one, but it was the queerest of goals.

I went up to head the ball, but did not connect with it properly. The goalkeeper completely misjudged it, however, and the ball rolled into the net.

That was my first Arsenal goal—one I could scarcely feel proud about.

I stayed at centre-forward, and on the following Boxing Day made my League debut at Stoke. The pitch was icy, and it wasn't a joyful start.

We were losing 1—0 when Peter Goring, playing at inside-right, crossed the ball. *I shot from two yards, and hit the goalkeeper on the chest.*

The ball cannoned over the bar, and a golden chance was lost. A goal then would have saved a point.

When a thing like that happens in your first big game, you remember it all through your career.

A lot has happened since then. There was the unforgettable Cup Final of 1952.

Newcastle beat us by a single goal from George Robledo after Walley Barnes, our right-back, had left the field, injured, in the 34th minute.

It was not until the day before the match that I was selected to play.

My display that day was one of my worst ever. For this reason I'm anxious to put things right—in another Wembley Cup Final.

I have since switched to wing-half, and really don't mind where I play. I'll admit to a sneaking regard for the centre-half position, but as long as I can hold a place in the first team, I'm quite happy.

GEORGE SWINDIN . . . he accidentally knocked out Holton who was going for his first ball in his first match for Arsenal.

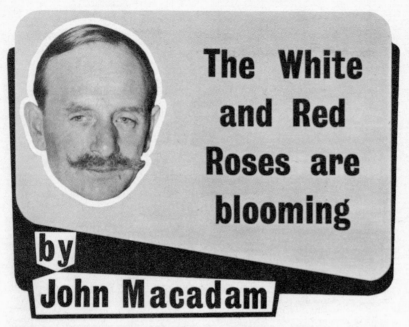

The White and Red Roses are blooming

by John Macadam

THE War of the Roses is over at last—at least, so far as Arsenal are concerned. Manager George Swindin is a Yorkshireman and his recently-appointed assistant manager, Ron Greenwood, is a Lancastrian.

Never the twain shall meet? On the contrary, they meet very happily every working morning in the Highbury dressing-rooms, and the association of these two men is the real reason for Arsenal's phenomenal revival.

It seems only yesterday that the once-great club were struggling in the League doldrums. Now they are freely tipped for the championship.

How this has been achieved is a matter of interest not only to Arsenal fans but to executives of every club in the country, for I believe the Swindin-Greenwood partnership is headed for greatness on a par with that of Matt Busby and Jimmy Murphy, of Manchester United.

George Swindin, fresh from his triumphant handling of non-League Peterborough, states the case with Yorkshire directness:

"When I came to Highbury, Ron was already doing a grand job on the youngsters' football. We have known each other for a long time and have a mutual respect and regard.

"So I leave him free to get on with his football coaching while I get on with the administration of the club's affairs."

But what we used to call admin-bashing is only a part of the Swindin job. His major task is to give the club leadership and confidence.

The impact of his tremendous vitality was apparent almost overnight.

Players who were hesitant, almost unbelieving of their own ability, shook off the shackles of despondency under the downright direction of this quietly buoyant man, and went about their work with a new zest.

"Of course, we are bound to come unstuck once in a while," he says with a rueful smile, "but the spirit is back there, and it is my job to keep it there.

"There has been too much talk about Tradition, too much living in the past and too much sorrowing for the past. I never look back . . . only forward. What happened yesterday is History. What happens tomorrow is News.

"LET'S FORGET ABOUT THE GREAT TRADITION. WE WILL MAKE OUR OWN!"

The old Arsenal style was to go for the quick goal and then go back into defence. Herbert Chapman perfected it, and he had Herbert Roberts around whom to build it.

But George Swindin doesn't believe in a playing policy based on defence.

"I believe in attack," he says. "Football is an entertainment—or ought to be. Unless we entertain, the crowds will stay away. Here, we plan to be entertaining—and *successful!"*

★

GEORGE SWINDIN . . . Arsenal players swear by him.

★

As to the success, only the end of the season will tell. Of the present entertainment, there is no doubt—any more than there is any doubt about the identity of the man who has galvanised Arsenal into it..

Swindin will have no part of the mustn't-lose attitude . . . "I believe only in the positive. The First Division of our League provides the toughest competition in the world and you cannot succeed in it today by negative football.

"You have to have the skill—and that's where Ron Greenwood comes in; to get the natural skills of the boys giving free expression. But you also have to have bite. Top-class football today is a hard, tough business, and only top-class practitioners can play in it.

"This is not to say that players must be dragooned. Just as I feel sometimes that there is too much playing *at* football, so I feel that we tend to forget the personality of the individual player.

"They are all individuals and they must be allowed to remain so.

"There are, of course, a few basic rules to be observed, and sometimes these rules, or some of them, have to be taught. But, that done, players should be left to themselves to develop their talents in their own way inside these basic principles.

"This is not anarchy. Most certainly we have tactical plans, but tactical plans are made to be changed. *If the plan isn't coming off on the field, then the players must have the personal equipment to modify it."*

Naturally enough, I wondered if Ron Greenwood's elevation to the Assistant Managership would affect his coaching activities, for there is no doubt that he is one of the best in the business.

I have spoken with many Arsenal players since his arrival and, to a man, they swear by him and his methods and the way he puts his message across.

There is no fear of his disappearance under a mass of replies to correspondents.

George Swindin, although occasionally he goes out on the field with the boys, is a very busy desk worker indeed, and leaves Ron free to get the playing part of the organisation just as they want it.

"We gave Ron the title," says Swindin, "to add official authority to his position. There is no truth in the suggestion that we elevated him to prevent his being lured away to other League clubs."

These two dedicated men have differences of opinion, of course, but their mutual appreciation allows them to iron such things out with the greatest smoothness. Normally, they dovetail completely.

"Often when we go to watch a player," says George, "we sit in different parts of the ground and compare notes afterwards. It is astonishing how often we find that we have come to the same conclusions.

"We have very similar views on the game. It all works out harmoniously. What we are trying to do at the moment is to find players and so order the staff that we can make room for the young ones.

"There's only one place to 'blood' a player—and that is on the field of play in match conditions.

"We have never been so understaffed. There are only thirty-six professionals on the books. That is not enough for Arsenal."

George Swindin's record is not a complicated one of shifts and starts. He joined Arsenal from Bradford City in 1936 and played for them eighteen years.

In 1954, he went to Peterborough as player-manager, stayed four years to make them the most-talked-of club outside the League, and returned to Highbury as manager in the summer of 1958. It is as simple as that.

Burnley-born Ron Greenwood was equally spare of movement. His clubs were Bradford, Brentford and Chelsea.

THE ONLY REAL DIFFERENCE BETWEEN THEM IS THE COLOUR OF THE ROSES THEY WEAR.

▲ March 1959

ARSENAL'S PETER GOY BELONGS TO OUR CLUB

★ ★

Dear Fellow-Members,

I expect many of you noticed that with both their regular goalkeepers injured, Arsenal gave a youngster named Peter Goy his First Division debut against Leeds United at Highbury on February 24.

Peter, who is 20 years old, gave a very promising display. As he gained confidence he made several very good saves. But the really interesting point about young Peter Goy is that HE IS ONE OF THE OLDEST MEMBERS OF OUR BOYS' CLUB.

In fact, his membership number is 1470, and I remember him particularly well because, back in March, 1952, Peter was chosen as our Soccer Boy of the Month. He was then thirteen years old.

At that time, Peter was keeping goal brilliantly for a club called Appleby-Frodingham Works Intermediate team, competing in an Under-18 League in his native Scunthorpe.

I recall that he was football crazy in those days. He played for his school team on Saturday mornings and for his club side in the afternoons. He was the youngest player appearing in the Under-18 League.

And even then, Peter's burning ambition was to join the Arsenal ground staff and bid for fame with the famous London club.

Well, Peter's wish came true and as I watched him in action under the Highbury floodlights, I wondered how many more of our members have managed to take the big step into League football, like Peter Goy.

Many professional footballers have been "Football Monthly" readers for a long while, we know, but it is very gratifying to find a club member taking his first confident steps up the ladder of Soccer success.

If you are offered the chance of a trial with a League club, please write and let me know so that I can pass on the good news to our readers.

I am sure you will join with me in wishing Peter Goy all the luck in the world with Arsenal. We shall be following his progress with great interest.

Until we meet here again, good luck to you all from

Sincerely yours,

Charles Buchan.

WIN A FINE FOOTBALL

THE letters from the surnames of five well-known international footballers have been arranged in this diagram on the left to form faces. We ask you to: 1, name these players; 2, name their clubs; 3, name the countries which they have represented.

Please remember to mark your entry with Comp. No. 86, your Club No., name and address.

The winner will receive a first-class football.

COMPETITION No. 84
Congratulations to David Matthews, of 20, Ludford Road, Bartley Green, Birmingham 32. David won Competition No. 84.

▲ May 1959

DENNIS EVANS (Arsenal)

DENNIS EVANS of Arsenal

recalls the time when he felt

A COMPLETE FOOL

ONCE I wanted to play for Everton . . . I might have become a Wolves man . . . but now I've settled down with the greatest club in the world . . . Arsenal. And had it not been for Harold Hassall, now manager-coach to the England Youth XI, I might not have become a professional at all.

Harold brought off a neat bit of 'kidding' which restored my confidence after I had broken my right leg in an Army Cup match at Tidworth.

I was doing my National Service in the Royal Artillery at Oswestry at the time. On the strength of my experience with South Liverpool, in the Cheshire County League, I had got into the regimental side, with Nigel Sims (then Wolves), Ian Jamieson (Coventry), Ivor Allchurch (Swansea, now Newcastle) and Harold Hassall.

Within three minutes of the start of our cup-tie I went down, writhing in agony, after a perfectly fair tackle.

It was thought at first that I had a severe strain, and they wanted me to go on the left-wing.

But when I tried to stand, it was hopeless. I was in hospital at Moston Hall, in Cheshire, for seven months.

I was worried about my leg for a long time, and thought I might not play again. One day I was doing some light training at Moston when Harold Hassall appeared. Casually he dropped a ball at my feet and told me to kick it as hard as I could.

As I swung my right foot, Harold suddenly blocked the ball—the impact was terrific. But I felt nothing. I knew I was O.K.

Back came all my old confidence, and within two weeks I was playing Soccer again for the Western Command. It was about this time that our goalkeeper, Nigel Sims, persuaded me to ask Wolves for a trial.

He said he could make arrangements—and he did. So, after I was demobbed, I went to Molineux for a week's training and coaching, and on the following Saturday appeared in Wolves' 'A' team against Tamworth, at right-half.

Frankly, I didn't have too good a game. I was advised by Wolves to go back to Liverpool and get more experience. So I returned to my native Merseyside and had a trial with Ellesmere Port as centre-half.

★

I played in the reserves for seven games, then was called for first-team duty at left-back. I settled down right away to this new position, had a fine first game, and became a regular in the side.

At school, during the war, I'd been a left-winger, but there wasn't much organised Soccer in those days, and I did not start playing regularly until 1946-47, with a team called Churchdown F.C. Then I had my trial with South Liverpool.

Four months after my successful conversion with Ellesmere Port, I heard that Arsenal were interested in me. I still fancied Everton as my club, but they had shown no interest at all.

My elder brother helped me make up my mind. "Go to Arsenal—they are a fine club," he advised. So on January 3, 1951, I was transferred to the famous London team for a fee of £1,500.

Life moved slowly but steadily after that. I spent twelve months in the 'A' team at Highbury, learning all the time, and then won a regular spot in the Football Combination team at left-back.

I was twelfth man for the first team in the opening game of the 1953-54 season, at West Bromwich, when Lionel Smith and Ben Marden were hurt.

The following Saturday, Gerry Ward and I made our League debuts together in a goalless draw against Huddersfield. Young Gerry, now doing so well at right-half, was on the left-wing.

He got the ball into the net—from an offside position. I gave him the pass, but had I slipped the ball through sooner, he would not have been offside and would have had the distinction of scoring in his first League match at 16. Sorry, Gerry!

We were both dropped soon afterwards, and not until the end of that season did I get another first-team chance.

Arsenal began the following campaign with Len Wills and Joe Wade as their full-back pair. Then Joe twisted a knee in a practice match, and I came in at left-back to play the remainder of the season.

From then on, I began to establish myself. In the 1955-56 season, I played in every game. The following year I appeared 37 times, and last winter lost my place only at the tail end.

I have not played in any other position than left-back since I have been an Arsenal man.

Which reminds me of an incident that made me look a complete fool but provided Highbury with one of its biggest laughs.

We were leading Blackpool 4—0 at Highbury, and I was right on top of the world . . . actually having a good game against Stanley Matthews.

About a minute from the end, someone in the crowd blew a whistle. We all thought it was time, and as I had the ball, about 30 yards from goal, I turned round and joyfully belted it towards our goalkeeper, Con Sullivan.

But he had picked up his cap and was walking off the pitch. The ball sailed past him into an empty net. To our amazement, the referee immediately blew his whistle and pointed to the centre spot for a goal.

It was not time by his watch, and so we had to play on another few seconds. If the scores had been level, or if we had been only a goal ahead when I took that happy-go-lucky kick, goodness knows what would have happened to Dennis Evans!

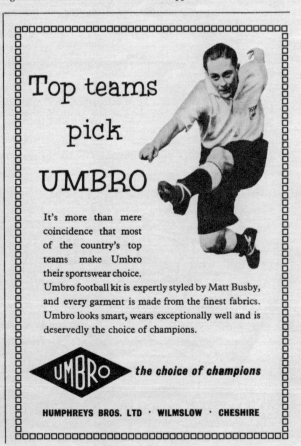
▲ April 1959

Two uneventful years in the Reserves, then from Highbury to my Army unit at Aldershot came . . .

MY PHONE CALL TO FAME

A PHONE call from Highbury to my Army unit at Aldershot changed my Arsenal career from one of doubtful uncertainty to first team success in a position I had never dreamt I could fill.

I had already made a shaky debut in Arsenal's League team at outside-left and had subsequently dropped back into the obscurity of the reserves when I got that call from assistant-coach George Male.

Arsenal wanted me to play right-half against Queen's Park Rangers in a London Challenge Cup match at Loftus Road. "Right-half? Very well . . . I'll have a go," I answered. I didn't mind where I played as long as I had a game.

I must have done well because Arsenal decided to carry on the experiment in the reserves for the remainder of the season. And I was given some pretty thorough coaching from those two former half-back stars Ron Greenwood and manager Jack Crayston.

Soon I found I really enjoyed this new position. Ron and Jack showed me the arts of linking up defence and attack and stressed the importance of getting the ball by determined tackling—the main job of any wing-half.

I was mindful, too, of the many fine wing-halves Arsenal have had on their books over the years and was anxious to try and do well.

In February, 1958, I received my first League chance at right-half at Highbury in a memorable match against Manchester United. Memorable . . . because it was the last First Division game United played before the terrible Munich air crash.

I kept my place in the side after that, and last season more or less established myself as the regular right-half following an injury to our skipper Dave Bowen.

And I apparently set up some sort of minor club

by GERRY WARD
of ARSENAL

record as a wing-half by scoring three goals in four games.

They came from shots just outside the penalty area and as a direct result of our tactical policy at Highbury which entails the half-backs closely following up the forwards when we are on attack.

Don't get me wrong—I have no great ambitions as a goalgetter. It just so happens I've been the man in possession when a shot has been "on". I've just been lucky enough to round off the moves developed by my colleagues.

Although wing-half is a comparatively new position for me as a professional, I have had some previous experience of the half-back line . . . but that takes me right back to my school days at Norlington Secondary Modern School in Leytonstone.

Which reminds me of a man who, outside Arsenal, has done more than anyone to help me. He is Mr. W. J. Saunders, sportsmaster at Norlington who virtually coached and cajoled me into the England schools side.

I was playing at centre-half in those days and Mr. Saunders apparently considered I was good enough for an international trial. But there were so many outstanding schoolboy centre-halves about that he decided I

▲ 1959–60 Gift Book

The Gerry Ward story might not have been so successful without the thorough coaching from former half-back stars Ron Greenwood (left) and Jack Crayston (right)

would stand a better chance of getting in as a left-winger.

His intuition proved correct. I played in a junior (under 14) trial at Chester and won a cap against Ireland at Bangor.

The next year I moved up into the England Under-15 team and was delighted to be chosen against Scotland in the big schools international at Wembley.

Again I was chosen at outside-left although I had been playing regularly for my school side at centre-half. This sort of thing happens quite often in schoolboy football where the biggest boys usually form the defence.

Following that Wembley game which was seen by many club scouts, I went one day to watch Arsenal play. I had always been something of a "Gunners" sup-

Gerry shows his mother how it's done

porter, along with my father and brothers, but had few chances to see the team in action. Anyway, I met Arsenal coach Alf Fields after that game and he arranged for me to see Jack Crayston. This was in 1952 and I had not reached my 16th birthday.

Eventually I was invited to sign amateur forms and I joined the Highbury ground staff where I played most of my soccer in the Eastern Counties League side under George Male.

At the start of the 1953 season, Ben Marden, the first team left-winger, got hurt at West Bromwich. On the Friday afternoon before our home game with Huddersfield, Mr. Tom Whittaker called me upstairs into his office and asked me if I had any qualms about playing outside-left for the League side the following day.

I tried hard not to be nervous but I couldn't help it. Arsenal were having a bad time of it just then and we weren't scoring any goals at home.

Suppose I missed an easy chance or something—right in front of our own supporters!

Well I didn't miss any chances and I did shoot the ball into the Huddersfield net. But the goal was disallowed for offside. The pass which gave me my chance had come from full-back Dennis Evans who was also making his Arsenal debut that afternoon.

We finished up 0—0 and Highbury fans were still moaning when the team was picked to visit Sheffield United the following Monday. I wasn't very prominent in this game which we lost by the only goal.

I was in the team again for the match at Villa Park and didn't feel too happy but Tom Whittaker gave me a lot of confidence. Then I lost form altogether and finished the season back in the reserves.

And there I stayed for two uneventful years until that fateful call to Aldershot gave me a new lease of life.

Probably the most notable match for me was my last as an amateur. Soon after my Arsenal debut I was selected for the England Amateur team to play Ireland at Coleraine. The following Monday I was 17 and signed professional forms for Arsenal.

Under Mr. George Swindin, I believe that Arsenal are once more heading for honours. There is no doubt that the famous Highbury club has a tremendous spirit. I can't hope to match my illustrious predecessors in ability but I hope I can in spirit.

ARSENAL F

Back row (left to right): LEN JULIANS, BILL McCULLOUGH, BILL DOD
PETTS; Middle row: JIMMY BLOOMFIELD, LEN WILLS, TOMMY DOCHE
Front row: JOHN BARN

C. 1959-60

M STANDEN, JACK KELSEY, MEL CHARLES, GERRY WARD, JOHN
IC GROVES, DAVID HERD, DANNY CLAPTON, JACK HENDERSON;
JOE HAVERTY.

by JIMMY MAGILL
Arsenal

ACROSS THE SEA TO FABULOUS HIGHBURY

NO one who lives in the little Northern Irish town of Lurgan thinks of it as a Soccer hotbed. But that is where I began a rather breathtaking journey which has landed me at Highbury with Arsenal—still one of football's glamour clubs in spite of recent ups and downs.

One of the big pleasures for me, of course, is the way in which I have been able to link up again with my old Portadown clubmate, Billy McCullough.

I took over from Billy at full-back in Portadown's Irish League team; now we have had the thrill of partnering each other for Arsenal in English First Division football!

Before that came about I had to play through the Carrick schoolboy team in Lurgan and thence to Portadown F.C.

It was not until I had been with Portadown for quite a time that I made my mark as a full-back. Until then I had been a centre-forward, a winger and a wing-half.

In 1952 I fancied myself as a centre-forward, especially as I had scored a fair quota of goals for my school.

My first job was as a textile worker in a Lurgan mill, and I joined the Edgarstown Boys' Club in nearby Portadown where I was still regarded as a centre-forward.

At 16, I was spotted by a Portadown official and I signed for them as an amateur.

At first I could not get more than a place in the third team, then I was promoted to the reserves—as a right or left-winger. I did not regard this as my best position.

I thought I could make a good job of the wing-half spot, although I played quite successfully in the first team on the wing.

But a try-out in the reserves at wing-half convinced the Portadown manager, Mr. Gibby MacKenzie, that I was a better defender than a forward, and he decided to give me a run at full-back.

At the beginning of the 1958-59 season I won a regular League place because the man I was to understudy,

Billy McCullough, was transferred to Arsenal.

To make room for me, our regular right-back was switched to the left flank and, in my first full season as a Portadown professional, I helped the team to finish in fourth place in the Irish League.

I had heard whispers that one or two English clubs were interested in me and I secretly hoped that Arsenal would make a move—if Portadown were willing to let me go to England.

Our shrewd manager kept me informed of developments and, although I was grateful to the Portadown club for the help they had given me, I was thrilled when I got an invitation to go for the first time across the Irish Channel to play a trial for Arsenal in a friendly match against Bath City.

This was an important game for me because the Arsenal manager, Mr. George Swindin, had not seen me play until then.

I knew he would be watching me carefully and I suppose I must have shown up fairly well because I was offered a professional engagement at Highbury soon after the Bath game.

I returned home for a short while to think things over, but really I was never in any doubt about accepting the chance to join the famous North London club. My parents had no objections, so on May 7, 1959, I returned to England and became an Arsenal professional.

One of the first to greet me was Billy McCullough and I soon learned to find my way round the magnificent Arsenal Stadium and to absorb the Arsenal club tradition.

On December 19, 1959, I made my first-team debut for Arsenal against Sheffield Wednesday at Hillsborough. The Wednesday were right at the top of their form just then and we knew we would be in for a tough game.

It was certainly not the ideal match for my debut, but I was determined to do my best.

Alas! The Wednesday were in fine fettle and they beat us 5—1.

I had the unenviable task of trying to mark their elusive left-winger and

captain, Alan Finney, who is almost as good a winger as was his famous namesake—in my opinion.

His intelligent switching and speed were more than anything I had then experienced, and I was mighty glad to hear the final whistle.

Mind you, we didn't have much good luck—Vic Groves was injured early in the game.

Probably my best first-team game last season was at Rotherham, in the F.A. Cup, where the Yorkshire Second Division team held us to a 2—2 draw.

Rotherham also forced another draw in the replay at Highbury and knocked us out of the Cup in a second replay—at Hillsborough!

I, for one, thought it poetic justice, when Rotherham, in turn, were knocked out of the Cup, also after a second replay, by Brighton—at Highbury!

Another dismal match for us was our 0—3 defeat by relegation-haunted Birmingham, last Easter.

Everything seemed to go wrong for us towards the end of last season, but none of us at Highbury intends to stay downhearted for long.

There is another campaign coming up and we shall all be making a fresh start with the idea of putting Arsenal back on top.

I believe it is a wonderful thing to be an Arsenal player.

Naturally, my greatest ambitions are to play for Northern Ireland and to appear at Wembley Stadium in an F.A. Cup Final.

High flown, maybe — but then, I never thought I would get as far in big Soccer as I have done.

The full-time training and specialised coaching I have received at Highbury has done my game a lot of good and, as I am only 20, I hope to improve still further next season.

I said that one of my ambitions is to play for my country.

Curiously enough, I have yet to meet my great boyhood idols, Peter Doherty and Danny Blanchflower, although Danny is only just up the road, as it were, at White Hart Lane, Tottenham.

HOME AND AWAY

This is the third in our series of articles on Soccer's 'top supporters'. This month an Arsenal Supporters' Club member puts the case for followers of The Gunners.
Watch for the club you follow . . .

IT has been said—without truth—that there are no *real* Arsenal supporters—only a crowd of cosmopolitan Soccer fans who go to Highbury because the ground is a mere ten-minute Tube ride from the West End of London!

As a very active member of the Arsenal F.C. Supporters' Club, I should like to let "Football Monthly" readers know something of the character and spirit of the Arsenal crowd as I see it at home and away.

And I'll begin by saying that I honestly believe Arsenal fans to be the most cheerful bunch in the game—either in victory or defeat.

There was a time, of course, when Highbury customers were brought up on victory and they were fully entitled to the view that they supported Britain's finest club side.

In recent seasons, I am afraid we Arsenal fans have had rather a lean time of it, but we still stay cheerful. Even when we lose by a last-minute goal, or finish up on the wrong end of a thrashing away from home, we can always raise a smile.

How many clubs possess supporters who can let rip with: "Two, four, six, eight, ten — blimey, Arsenal's lost again!" when their favourites go down to defeat? Not many, I should think.

Let me give you an instance. A couple of seasons ago I was one of a party of Arsenal supporters who travelled up to Molineux where the rampaging Wolves crushed us 6—1.

Were we downhearted? Not on your life! As our homeward-bound train pulled into Snow Hill Station, Birmingham, we were kicking up such a racket with bells and rattles that people on the platform who had not heard the result thought we had won!

One thing about it, there are always enough of us to make our presence felt—whether it be at Highbury, Cardiff, Preston or Newcastle.

by DAVID STACEY *

Last season Arsenal were the fifth best-supported club in the country, with average home crowds of 39,508—which was more than Burnley, the League champions, attracted, or Wolves, the F.A. Cup-winners. A big percentage of that 39,000 were genuine members of the Arsenal Supporters' Club who turn up week by week, rain or shine.

Many of them travelled thousands of miles to support Arsenal in away games and will be doing so again this season, trying hard to live up to their motto of 'Cheerful in defeat and modest in victory,' a phrase made famous by one of Arsenal's greatest-ever players, the late Charles Buchan.

Arsenal Supporters' Club, founded in August, 1949, now has a membership of over 20,000. It is still on the increase.

It is often a difficult task to try and foster sportsmanship between rival club supporters, and we Arsenal fans spare no effort to create good-will.

Often before a match, I parade round the ground with our Supporters' Club banner, inscribed 'May the Best Team Win.' I have done this on several grounds all over England and have always received grand co-operation from the

officials of the home club, for which I am very grateful.

Of course, I don't always get a good reception from the home fans. On occasions I have been pelted with orange peel, whistled and jeered at, and have a very uncomfortable tour round the cinder track. But most of it has been good humoured fun and I've worn the biggest smile of all.

Generally, I find that supporters up and down the country are a grand lot who are always willing to discuss football with you and will often go out of their way to provide hospitality when we visit their own club.

One such club is Manchester City, who have a Supporters' Club equally as active as our own and who give Arsenal club members a wonderful time whenever we visit Maine Road. We, in turn, are glad to reciprocate when City are down at Highbury. In the past we have had some grand Saturday evening socials with our friends from Manchester.

Other club supporters who stand out for fairness and sporting spirit are to be found at Portsmouth, Blackburn, Blackpool, Leicester, Sheffield and Colchester. They are all fine chaps and a credit to our great game.

I remember one Sheffield United supporter turning to me after Arsenal's Cup defeat last season and saying: "You had all the bad luck in having to play with ten men. I hope Arsenal will have a better run next season." That United fan was certainly being modest in victory.

Now to explode another fallacy . . . as far as Arsenal are concerned, anyway.

While it may be true that many foot-

Continued

HOME and AWAY

Continued

ball club directors have little contact with their supporters' clubs and seem virtually to ignore their existence, the Arsenal board and officials keep in close touch with us all through the year.

Two incidents will illustrate what I mean. One Easter we travelled to Wolverhampton and lost 2—1 after a terrific fight by our boys, who were encouraged by our cheers from the terraces.

On the train back, we found on our table in the dining car a bottle of champagne. It was marked 'With the compliments of Arsenal F.C.'

On another occasion, several of our younger members were treated to morning coffee on the train by Commander Bone, one of the Arsenal directors. They were not aware at first that he was indeed an Arsenal official, but once they were told, the lads could not find words enough to thank him for his kindness.

It is the little personal touch like this that makes the association between Arsenal supporters and the parent club such a happy one.

Of course, no Arsenal supporter will be content to watch the club play mediocre football for long. We still dream with nostalgia of the days of James, Jack, Bastin, Copping, Crayston and the great names of the 1930's.

Even in the post-war years, there have been a galaxy of names to inspire us, like Ronnie Rooke, Joe Mercer, Walley Barnes, Jimmy Logie and the Compton brothers, just to mention a few.

We have to take a 'ribbing' from supporters of the other big London clubs like Chelsea, West Ham, Fulham, and our most formidable rivals, Tottenham Hotspur.

The White Hart Lane contingent have had plenty to shout about, and it is true to say that their club has been pulling in most of the Soccer fans in North London.

I make no secret of the fact that there *IS* rivalry between the two sets of supporters at Tottenham and Highbury, just as there has always been rivalry between these two powerful League clubs whose homes are so close together in densely populated North London.

But a lot of the bitterness of former years has happily disappeared, and nowadays Arsenal fans will often go to White Hart Lane when the Highbury first team is away, and Tottenham followers make the short journey across to watch Arsenal when there is no League game at White Hart Lane.

I believe there is an 'atmosphere' at Highbury on match-days which cannot be duplicated at any other League stadium. Each ground has its own special atmosphere, and at Highbury it is of London and the Londoners.

Especially is it of the red and white of the 'Gunners', perhaps the most famous of all the League clubs in the metropolis, to whose wonderful legion of supporters I am proud to belong.

*IN AN INTERVIEW WITH PETER MORRIS.

FEW of the television watchers who saw Denmark beaten by Yugoslavia in the Olympic Games Soccer final last month, and applauded the clever play of the gallant Danes, would know that the first football ever seen in Denmark was a birthday present!

The father of an English boy who was at a Danish public school —the Soro academy—sent the ball as a gift to his son in 1879.

Within a week it was kicked to pieces by the enthusiastic boys. But in the same year, the headmaster at another school introduced the English game and it was adopted by Denmark's oldest sports club— Copenhagen Boldklub.

That was the start of organised Soccer in Denmark. In the next 20 years several clubs were formed in Denmark and league matches were played, although the game remained in a rather primitive state.

In 1898, Queen's Park, Glasgow, came over to show the Danes just how football *should* be played. Their visits were repeated in 1900 and 1903 and, from 1904 onwards, prominent British clubs visited Denmark every year.

Before this year's final, Denmark had reached the Olympic finals in 1908 and 1912.

NILS MIDDLEBOE
(former Danish international and Chelsea F.C. full-back).

Show them you can become a husky he-man

IN 7 DAYS I'LL PROVE YOU CAN BE PROUD OF YOUR BODY!

Don't let others take the "mickey" out of you because of your skinny build! Give me seven days and I'll prove that you'll add powerful **NEW MUSCLE** so fast your friends will gape with wonder! I don't dose or doctor you. And I've no use for weights and other contraptions that may strain your vital inner organs.

"DYNAMIC-TENSION" DOES IT
All I want you to do is apply my famous "Dynamic-Tension" to the "sleeping" muscle power in your own body. In only 15 minutes a day you'll soon notice an amazing difference. Your shoulders begin to swell, you add inches to your chest, strengthen your back, give yourself a vicelike grip and mighty legs that never get tired! My free 32-page book tells all about "Dynamic-Tension"—the natural method which changed me from a skinny weakling to **twice** winner of the title: "The World's Most Perfectly Developed Man." It shows what I'll do for **YOU**! Post coupon at once to:

CHARLES ATLAS
Dept. 190-L, Chitty Street, London, W.1.

SEND FOR MY *FREE* BOOK

CHARLES ATLAS
Dept. 190-L, Chitty Street, W.1
Send me absolutely **FREE** and without obligation a copy of your Famous Book "You, Too, Can Be a New Man" and details of your amazing **7-DAY TRIAL OFFER**

NAME.................................... AGE.........
(Capital letters please)
ADDRESS ....

Here's the kind of body I want!
(Check as many as you like)

☐ More weight—solid —in the right places.
☐ Broader chest and shoulders.
☐ Slimmer waist and hips.
☐ Better regularity, digestion, clear skin.
☐ More powerful leg muscles.
☐ Better sleep, more energy.

Charles Buchan's FOOTBALL MONTHLY

OCTOBER 1961

Overseas Price 2/–
Forces Overseas 1/6

1/6

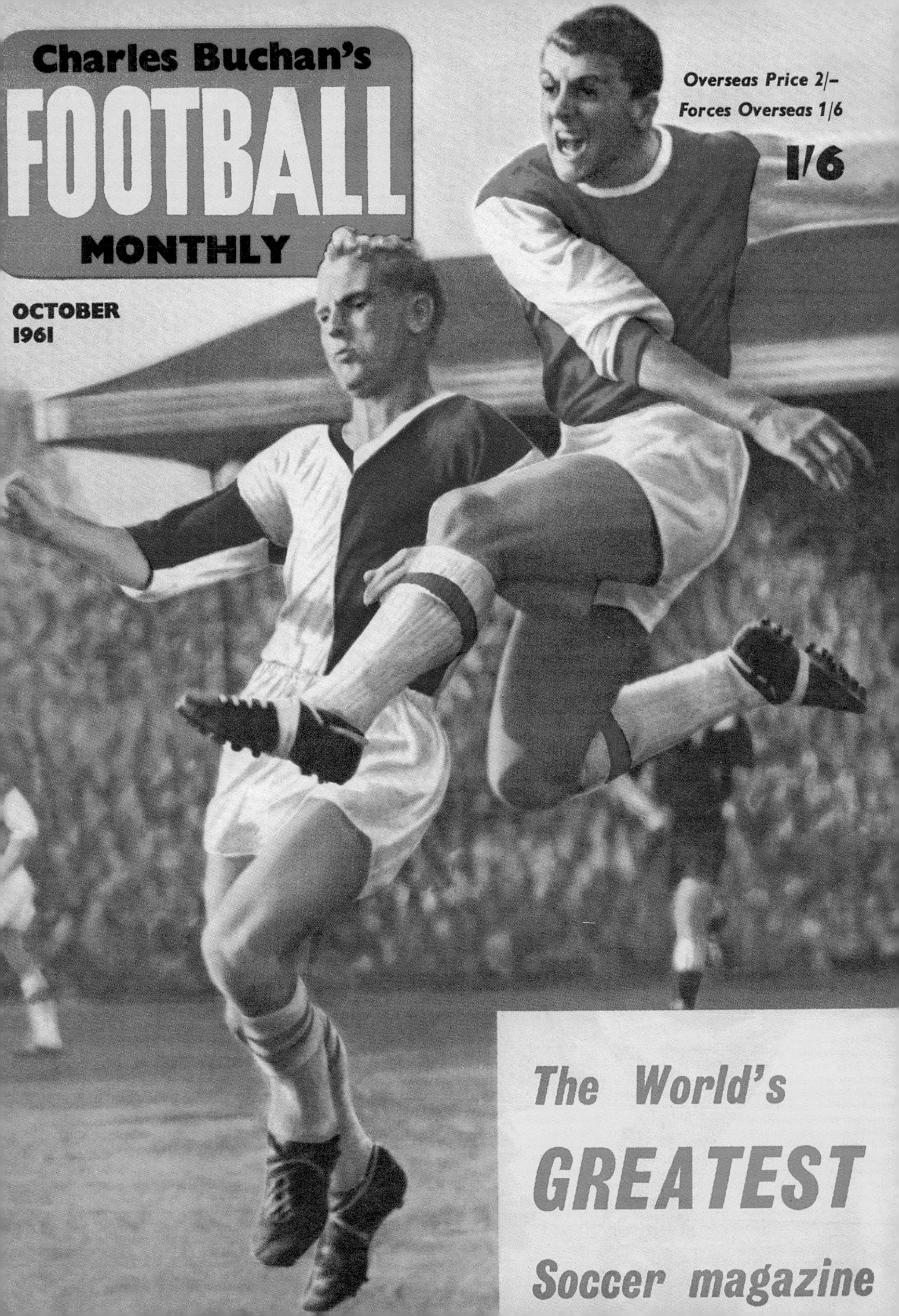

The World's GREATEST Soccer magazine

Rebel George Eastham poses in front of the bust of the

With secretary Bob Wall.

THE New Gunner! George Eastham, the winner of the longest one-man strike in the history of football, stands on the inlaid emblem of Arsenal, in the marbled hall of Highbury Stadium (top left). Eastham, who for 140 days had refused to play for his club, Newcastle United, was transferred in November 1960, for £47,500. We show him on his first two days with The Gunners.

Top right—in action again! Only a day after joining Arsenal, Eastham was given a run-out with their reserves—watched by young and not so young, fans.

▲ 1961–62 Gift Book

greatest Arsenal manager of them all—Herbert Chapman

The game is over. Eastham now faces requests for his autograph—including one from Graham Quick, who is wearing the rig of Newcastle United. He is their mascot.

Here is one good reason why Arsenal paid £62,500 to Dundee for Scotland centre-half Ian Ure. Against Wolves he was in the thick of it all the time, and here he is soaring high above Laurie Brown (No. 6), Terry Wharton (No. 7) and goalkeeper Jack McClelland, to check a shot.

Geoff Strong (Arsenal) has Sid
Bishop (Leyton Orient) well covered.
In background, Alan Skirton (Arsenal).

◀ November 1963 | November 1962 ▲

the old

Arsenal of the mid-twenties: Standing—Cope, Baker, Parker, Lewis, Butler, John, Kennedy, Seddon. Sitting—T. Whittaker (then trainer), Hulme, Buchan, Brain, Blythe, Hoare, H. Chapman (manager).

ARSENAL—a name you feel you

WHEN one speaks or writes the name Arsenal there is an uncomfortable feeling that it should be done standing up.

Loved or hated fiercely as they have been across the last 30-odd years there is still an unmistakable ring about that name. It is a royal salute by gunfire.

It was on the open north terrace at Highbury in the winter of 1929 that my eyes were first opened to the magic and poetry of football.

I had always loved the game from earliest youth. But in one sudden moment that wet afternoon long ago the sheer wonder of it struck home. It was done in a twinkling.

Sheffield United were the visitors.

They opened the scoring early on. Then came the lightning. The blinding flash was provided by wee Alex James, the genius, recently arrived from the north.

As a fast, through pass out of defence cut down the middle, James flitted across its line, waved a foot over the ball, letting it go on its path unhindered.

The full effect was achieved without so much as a touch. It was like the waving of a conjuror's wand.

The whole Sheffield defence was mesmerised and wrong footed; a wide avenue opened up like magic and through it strolled Lambert with the ball to stroke home the equaliser.

From that moment the Yorkshiremen were cut to pieces as Arsenal swept gloriously to an 8—1 victory. Yet all that my memory still hugs is that feint, that decoy, by James. It was the beginning of education.

Soon after that the name of Arsenal went round the world. They became as famous in Finland, in Greenland, in Chile, in China, as in North London.

Clubs, even small amateur growths in hamlets, copied their red colours.

They became a by-word as team after team, even national sides overseas, imitated—or tried to—their new defensive system of the

stopper centre-half invented in 1926 by Herbert Chapman, their famous manager, and Charles Buchan, their reigning captain, to counter the recent change in the off-side law.

It was Herbert Chapman who became the true architect of the Arsenal of modern times.

Having earlier made Huddersfield Town the colossus of English football, he now achieved the trick at Highbury so that he became the master tactician and the dominating single link between the 1920s and 1930s.

Yet by their very dominion of those great days Arsenal aroused a mountain of jealousy in small-minded people.

The North had its nose out of joint

The North, in particular, found its nose put out of joint. "Lucky Arsenal" became the parrot cry as the suspicion grew that here were merely the *nouveau riche* of a changing world, living on cheap publicity.

How the years have proved them all wrong! There have been good times since those days, but many bad times, too. Yet Arsenal have proved themselves, through thick and thin, no bubble to be easily pricked.

Over three decades is an ocean of time to remain buoyant in the pressure cooker of modern football, where success usually has lasted only over midnight and where new idols swiftly take the place of the old.

A strong Arsenal has always been good for the English game: that, at least, is the opinion of all fair-minded people. And now at this moment, after five lean years of flattering hopes and disappointments, the flag of Arsenal—of "The Gunners"—is fluttering again near the top of the mast.

New triumphs may be just around the corner, though whether they will ever again match the battle honours of the past is arguable.

The character of great clubs is formed by the atmosphere of the district in which they play, by the spirit of those who support them, and by those who mould them. Britain's most distinguished football writer, GEOFFREY GREEN, in this article, captures the character of ARSENAL.

▲ February 1964

Arsenal in the middle of 1963: Outside the Highbury ground their (then) latest signing, Scottish centre-half, Ian Ure, is mobbed by young autograph-hunters.

should utter only when standing

It is all a matter of age. To youth it is today that counts: to their elders the nostalgia of yesterday lingers on strongly. Whatever the raging, endless arguments over comparisons — present tactics, methods and skills measured against the past—one thing remains.

Even mere utility is granted a special quality by the Arsenal tradition, a quality that still keeps the club its glorious and hard-won position in the opinions of those who must face it.

Part of this tradition is that seldom does a man who joins Highbury want to leave. That in itself is significant.

Contemporary Arsenal, man for man, may not truly measure up to some of the giants of the past. Yet in George Eastham, the sensitive creator with the high-stepping stride and the frail-looking legs; the darting Baker of the swift shot, wisely recovered from Italy at a cost of £70,000 in 1962; Strong, long of limb with spring heels and a deadly header; the tall Scotsman Ure, bought this season for £62,500 to be the new centre piece of defence . . . there are men who might well have fitted into any Arsenal combination of other days.

Tactically, too, the years seem to have wrought a change.

Modern way is attack — which is life!

Once, Arsenal were famed for their defensive rampart built around the red head of Herbert Roberts, the original "stopper" centre-half sired by Chapman. Many were the matches Arsenal won by the snatched goal after having seemingly defended for 75 per cent of the afternoon.

That was the birth of the cry "Lucky Arsenal"—though the goals scored over a period scarcely support that proposition—127 in 1930-31; 118 in 1932-33; 115 in 1934-35.

Today, the Arsenal philosophy seems to be, "if you can score three, we can get four." It is healthy. That is attack, which is life.

Yet in 1932-33 Bastin's League bag alone was 33 goals—still a record for a winger—and Hulme's 20. In all, they each scored 150 and 108 times respectively in Arsenal League matches, although it is true that Bastin, great player that he was, often appeared at inside-left.

Arsenal have had two great spells in their life. Between 1926 and 1938 they reached the Cup Final four times (twice victoriously); the semi-final once; and the last eight on five other occasions.

In addition, they won the League title five times in eight years—thrice in succession to equal the earlier record of Huddersfield—besides being runners-up and third in that same remarkable spell.

Later, between 1948 and 1953, they again caught the tide, reaching Wembley twice (with victory over Liverpool), and taking the League twice more to create another record.

Such are their marks of distinction. More perhaps are on the way under the guidance of Billy Wright, upon whom the mantle of famous Chapman, George Allison, Tom Whittaker and others has fallen.

Yet facts and figures are only the skeletons of the story. It was men who provided the flesh and blood, the pride and the team spirit that have become the pillars of Arsenal's fame.

What a great cavalcade they make! The long-legged Charles Buchan, around whose attacking skill (plus the defensive centre-half) Chapman laid the foundations of fame; Hulme, whose speed brought the crowds tumbling down the terraces; the immortal, unorthodox Alex James with the baggy pants and the puckish humour in his educated feet; Bastin, the boy who found maturity beyond his years, detached, ice-cool, sheer destruction in his left foot.

There were Hapgood and Male, forming one of England's greatest full-back partnerships; David Jack, all consummate grace; and Ted Drake.

Later there came Walley Barnes, Logie, the Compton brothers, and Joe Mercer, of the crablike legs, a great competitor and leader of men. The list is endless, but there it must stop.

Arsenal today remain a monument, one of the prides of North London, a place where millions have made their pilgrimage.

September 1963

CHARLES BUCHAN'S

FOOTBALL

MONTHLY

DECEMBER, 1963

The World's Greatest Soccer Magazine

2/-

OVERSEAS PRICE 2/6
FORCES OVERSEAS
2/-

INSIDE: GREAT COLOUR PICTURES
AND STORIES BY THE STARS

JOE BAKER
(Arsenal and England)

Star Strip — GEORGE EASTHAM

◄ 1963–64 Gift Book | July 1965 ▲

ARSENAL: Standing—Graham, Addison, McLintock, Furnell, Storey, Simpson, McNab. Sitting—Neilson, Armstrong, Neill, Ure, Sammels.

ARSENAL

I BECAME an Arsenal supporter while a schoolboy in Berlin. I had started to go to football matches after an uncle had taken me to the new Olympic Stadium in 1936.

However, notices soon went up around all German football grounds saying: "Dogs and Jews are not allowed to enter here"; I was sensitive and sensible enough not to follow the example of some of my friends who watched matches illegally, and despite the notices.

But I was addicted to football and, by following newspaper reports, I started to identify myself with Arsenal.

Why Arsenal? Possibly because they played with a consistent style or method which gave me a chance to visualise them playing, without ever having seen them in real life.

Another reason was the Arsenal colours, red and white. They were distinctive and different, and in the Germany of those dark years those particular colours were regarded as revolutionary and undesirable.

Thus, my interest in Arsenal became an essential escape from the rather unpleasant reality surrounding me. Not only did it help me to stay sane, but the Arsenal of those pre-war years also instilled in me a love for football, not only as a game of natural skills but as an exercise in tactical thought and method.

I could add a whole chapter on the day I saw Arsenal play for the first time. Suffice to say that I had no difficulty in recognising the various players from my lonely, escapist newspaper reading . . .

Only they looked much bigger and played even better than the figments of my imagination!

ADAM BEN-CHANOCH,
360 Finchley Road, London, N.W.3.

▲ May 1966 | April 1967 | April 1967

ON PARADE! THE GUNNERS (1967-68) IN BATTLE DRES

Back row: Neilson, Addison, Woodward, Simpson, Wilson, Furnell, Howe, McLintock, Graham, Johnston, Armstrong.
Front: Storey, McNab, Sammels, Ure, Neill, Court, Radford, McGill, Coakley.

THE TARNISHED IMAGE

**ARSENAL
... will they
really mean
something
this season?**

asks PETER MORRIS

LOUD noises from Highbury in August indicated that Arsenal were going through their annual muscle-flexing and trumpeting well-meant intentions of making their long awaited come-back.

This threat was emphasised when they kicked off with four sparkling victories—one against the league champions no less—leaving only the sceptics to point out that it had happened before and Arsenal had failed to sustain their premature role of pacemakers.

These days, it is not always clear whether Arsenal believe they can really challenge for the League title or whether they merely want to regain their place as London's top club and leave it at that.

In this matter of Metropolitan parochialism Arsenal have long relinquished the leadership to the ambitious upstarts from West Ham and Chelsea and those crusty old rivals at White Hart Lane who are slouching a bit themselves nowadays.

I doubt if Arsenal have ever believed they were inviolate; that the palmy days of Chap-

man and Allison would go on forever.

But their retreat from glory has been, in the main, a bitter one, soured by a prolonged diet of non-success after so much of it; bedevilled by unfortunate managerial appointments and squalid disputes with players.

Too much of the old Arsenal pride has been sabotaged from within, too much of the respect in which they were once universally held has withered away when it should not have done.

In the provinces, in the 1930s, they made a fetish of hating Arsenal, exulting in their defeat. In those days Arsenal were symbolic of a so-called glittering glamorous pre-war London on the other side of the world it seemed. But always, they won respect.

Now, of course, that northern spleen is spent, Arsenal are no longer larger than life but often left peeping about between the feet of the northern Soccer colossus.

No use looking to the past. The Jacks and the Jameses have passed into history and all the others overtaken by time and motion.

Bernard Joy, distinguished

Soccer correspondent of the London Evening Standard, himself once one of Arsenal's pre-war elite, writes in the club programme of "tradition with a barb in the tail."

Arsenal, with unbroken membership of the First Division since 1919—the whole of the modern football era in truth—have that tradition. It is a heritage shared by only a few clubs.

But the barb in the tail has stung rather than stimulated more often than not. And in Arsenal's case the sting of failure has been intense since 1953 when they last won the League championship — their seventh, a record shared to date by only Manchester United and Liverpool.

When Tom Whittaker, the remaining link with Herbert Chapman, passed on, the managerial chair, so comfortable in Chapman's heyday and that of his successor, George Allison, became increasingly "hot".

In turn, Jack Crayston, George Swindin and Billy Wright found the mantle of Chapman's greatness of suffocating weight.

Crayston, former England wing-half with the club, was perhaps too much of a gentleman to grapple successfully with ever increasing pressures on his good nature; Swindin, another ex-playing stalwart, uncompromising to the point of extreme toughness, found a new type of Arsenal player resenting measures his own contemporaries had accepted; and Wright, the golden boy of Wolves and England with no Arsenal connections whatsoever and a learner-manager into the bargain, was given too much too soon.

Like Swindin, he too, discovered he was short of the brave hearts he had been accustomed to at Molineux and was entitled to expect at Highbury.

For a brief while, during Tom Whittaker's time, Arsenal took on Alec Stock as assistant-manager. But Stock was too much of an individualist to fall in easily with the old Highbury ways. He followed his own star with outstanding success.

With luck, he could have

Right: BERTIE MEE ... the present boss—he can seldom draft in a youngster

Facing page: BILLY WRIGHT ... given too much too soon

◀◀ December 1967

▲ October 1968

been just the man for Arsenal. So, too, could Ron Greenwood who also found success after leaving Highbury.

To my mind, one of the most significant weaknesses at Highbury in recent years has been the club's seeming inability to discover and develop into First Division players their own youngsters.

Always, or nearly always, they have had to enter the transfer market to strengthen a sometimes dreadfully inept team.

Of their 40-strong playing staff for this season only four professionals and one apprentice are London-born. And of these, only David Court has had first team experience so far. In fact, last season he made just 15 League appearances. The remainder are from every corner of the British Isles and even from Accra (Ghana).

This diversity of origin is not peculiar to Arsenal. But unlike other First Division clubs, Arsenal have rarely found the right material on their own doorstep. They have paid small fortunes for established stars but, then, they have never needed to do otherwise. So far . . !

Some of the current Arsenal staff have developed their football in London but they are a minority.

It is hard to accept that a club of Arsenal's calibre can find no pickings among the rich and varied football life to be found in the streets, playgrounds and parks of teeming north London. The

Spurs have spotted a few from time to time in their own "manor" but it has been left largely to Chelsea and West Ham to milk London of boys of such tremendous potential that one can only wonder about the efficiency of Arsenal's scouting system.

Perhaps Arsenal could also learn a thing or two from the Queen's Park Rangers' talent spotters.

All this means that Arsenal's present manager, Bertie Mee, must pay a sizable fee whenever he needs to strengthen his side. He can seldom draft in a youngster as Manchester United, West Ham, Burnley and others, even the reputedly high-spending Everton, have done so successfully and so often.

And now, on their own admittance, via their chairman, Mr. Denis Hill-Wood, Arsenal plead they have difficulty in buying the players they want.

No longer is the famed Highbury cheque book the instrument of success. In the old days Arsenal invariably got the man they wanted—David Jack, Bryn Jones and so on. But offers to clubs soaring upwards of £125,000 a few months ago brought only outright refusals or a player-exchange demand.

More disturbing were the pre-season transfer requests of Frank McLintock and Jon Sammels who considered Arsenal's chances of success to be doubtful. Times have certainly changed when an Arsenal star wants away for this reason alone. Bertie Mee's

managerial spell so far at Highbury has certainly been no sinecure.

He has been plagued by injuries and transfer requests, is in danger of losing his best wing-half and the only genuine mid-field ball-player since George Eastham, and has come in for probably more than his fair share of criticism from supporters and shareholders.

Yet he has kept his side in the First Division with some degree of comfort and has fashioned a formidable defence in which the influence of chief coach, Don Howe, former England full-back *par excellence* is also evident.

Mee, a skilled coach himself, has based his faith this season on a solid 4-3-3 formation emphasised by the power of Neill and Simpson (and Ure on his return after injury), the poise of McLintock and the determination of Radford and the ball-carrying industry of Sammels.

His side have heart and willingness to work—more so than some recent Arsenal sides have demonstrated—but they lack attacking penetration. This was never more cruelly exposed than in last season's

League Cup Final against Leeds.

Last season, Mee elevated eyebrows and pursed lips when he paid out £90,000 for Coventry's Bobby Gould, a young centre-forward who appeared to possess little else apart from the ability to pop in valuable goals for Coventry during their promotion run.

But Gould's knack is a priceless one and this he proved immediately on his recall to the side in the second match of the season. Should George Graham also recapture his Chelsea form, then Mee may find he will not need to buy after all.

Whatever else, in what may be an uplifting season for the "Gunners", there is unlikely to be any complacency at Highbury this year.

Perhaps, too, we will see some Arsenal-raised youngsters coming off the assembly line into the First Division.

This will be a new and refreshing thing to behold. For in this era of inflated transfer fees dominating an often lunatic market, Arsenal's cash is no better than the next club's when it comes to buying current success.

GEORGE GRAHAM
Arsenal

Spearheading Arsenal's success and on the fringe of full England status

JOHN RADFORD

talks to Peter Morris

IT'S hard to spot him off-field as the strong-running, hard-shooting personality player currently thrilling the Highbury crowd. He looks a lot slimmer, a lot paler, for one thing, and the fierce aggression so evident in Arsenal's raging attack this season is simply not there.

This John Radford who so nearly made the England team against Bulgaria before Christmas is a soft-spoken character, quite unlike some of his footballing fore-bears from South Yorkshire who were hard cases indeed, both on and off the field.

As yet, he hasn't taken on the fashion-able trappings of the 1969 star-player-type. He is a modest fellow, almost self-deprecatory in talking of his career which began humbly enough with a local youth team in his native Hemsworth, near Pontefract. But make no mistake, John Radford is worth his weight to Arsenal

these days. As a front-runner, along with George Armstrong and Bobby Gould, he is giving close-packing defences a little more than they can cope with in most matches.

In seasons 1966-67 and 67-68 he scored only 21 goals in Football League, League Cup and F.A. Cup games. Then he was operating mostly as an inside-right. This season, at the time of writing, he had already netted 13 in League and League Cup, plus another one for England's Under 23 side since being switched to the right-wing.

"But," he says, "I'm not really a winger I have the freedom to roam any-where and no definite commitments."

His contribution towards Arsenal's feat of reaching the League Cup Final for the second year running and simul-taneously mounting the strongest title challenge from Highbury for many seasons has been invaluable.

None more so than his League Cup semi-final goals against Spurs this season. He got the only one at Highbury and the equaliser at White Hart Lane which put Arsenal through on 2-1 aggregate and sent their fans into a delirium of madness (and near mayhem).

Radford rates these goals the most memorable of his career to date—even transcending the hat-trick he hit inside five minutes against Bolton in the League Cup last season and another he collected against Wolves in only his third League game for the Gunners some three-and-a-half years ago.

A strong player in the air with heading powers of accuracy and timing as good as anyone in the business, Radford is notably dangerous with either foot off half-chances in the six yard box and beyond.

"*You must be looking for shooting chances all the time in the six yard box. That's where most of the goals come,*" he explains.

Yet the season before last he admits, "*I could hardly get a goal . . . in fact none of us could.*"

So why the exciting transformation?

"*It's hard to put a finger on it . . . I suppose both manager Bertie Mee and coach Don Howe have exerted the influence although we've got much the same players.*"

Certainly Arsenal have shaped into the best side Radford has played with in his six years with the club and already more away games have been won than in the whole of last season.

Arsenal's job has not been made easier by the manner in which the current back-slide to defensive football is choking and frustrating attackers all over the country.

Says Radford: "*For instance, we are finding it a lot harder to break through in our home games. Some teams are bringing back eight or nine men into their penalty area—just to play for a point. We are always going for a win although in away games we, too, have to concentrate more on defence than on attack—but that's the way it usually is. The difference is that we are mounting incisive attacks from a defensive position and if we can make three good chances from our counter attacks we are perhaps taking two of them. It's often enough to win us the game,*" he explained.

But Radford deplores the defensive complex. "*If both sides are playing attacking football you are bound to see a good game,*" he says.

He instanced the Arsenal-Everton match before Christmas when both sides thrilled a 40,000 crowd with exhilarating attacks—a game which Arsenal won only because, on the day, they were more adroit in taking chances than an Everton who set up almost as many.

"*Liverpool and Manchester United are two more teams who are always willing to come to you even when they are playing away,*" he says.

Radford, now an integral part of Arsenal's machine in the new drive for success, takes particular delight in playing against Manchester United.

"*As a kid I supported them and I hoped one day to play for them but they never came for me so that was that.*"

Now on the fringe of the England team —and surely it must be only a matter of time—John Radford owes much of his success to two people. The sportsmaster who switched him from centre-half to centre-forward in his school team and Chelsea manager Dave Sexton who spent so much time helping Arsenal's young forwards, of which Radford was one, during his Highbury coaching days.

Both can share some credit for spotting an England player of the future. So, too, can Arsenal for perservering with him as an apprentice at a time when they were inclined to be overloaded.

RADFORD (far right) opens scoring in Highbury classic against Everton

◀ October 1968 | February 1969 ▲

Swindon may ram these lines
back in my teeth, SAYS PAT COLLINS,
but I forecast...

IT WILL BE ARSENAL'S

THE time does come when one can in all honesty make out a case for an upset in form; a time when a team of lesser station besting one from way higher is definitely on. It is good that this can be so.

But with all the goodwill in the world, and bending over backwards (dangerously so), I cannot see Third Division Swindon, decked out in their new all-white strip for the occasion, taking the shine out of the golden garb of Arsenal at Wembley on March 15.

I confidently anticipate Arsenal captain Frank McLintock, who has had to stand back and make way for the winners on three other Wembley occasions, leading the way to the Royal Box to receive the Football League Cup.

It would be deserved personal compensation for McLintock being a Leicester runner-up in FA Cup Finals against Spurs and Manchester United, and in Arsenal's League Cup defeat by Leeds last year.

Swindon Town have heroically arrived at the Stadium for the first time, an appearance magnificently earned. *But the dispatching of Burnley in those three, taut,*

tingling semi-final games will, I feel, still rate as their greatest achievement at the end of the day.

Swindon's history is homely and ordinary—two seasons in the Second Division being their League high-spots, and two semi-final appearances way back in 1910 and 1912, the heyday of Harold Fleming, their greatest Cup moments.

Arsenal's, by comparison, is profusely pitted with glamorous landmarks which take in League championships and Wembley Cup victories.

An upset of the odds on March 15 would surely set the sculptured figure of Fleming, that once great man, spinning on its pedestal in the forecourt of the County Ground. But you won't hear a

Wiltshire burr from now to Wembley which says other than victory for Danny Williams' boys.

They can make out a case . . . the defeats of Blackburn, of Coventry and Derby where Swindon first had to go and hold out at Highfield Road and the Baseball Ground; in particular, the defeat of Burnley.

They cheekily, but convincingly won at Turf Moor, then fell at home. It was a prelude to the most breathless, most heart-stopping match for seasons. The sort which, if it were possible to guarantee, would need half a dozen Wembley Stadiums to house the customers.

Town tackled then a reviving Burnley team of talented youngsters giving visions of recapturing the high-days at Turf Moor.

Danny Williams, and his directors, have their eyes on the big prize for Town . . . promotion. It will mean more than Wembley in the long run. But priorities will be switched for the day when Stan Harland leads out his men against the Gunners.

Swindon's strength, like Arsenal's, is in well-ordered, highly disciplined strength at the back. Frank Burrows, bought from Scunthorpe, has proved a canny Williams buy. *And he has bought none better than Harland.*

His full-backs, from among Owen Dawson, Norman Trollope and Welsh international Rod Thomas, having his finest season yet, won't let Town down.

Then there is the deep-lying John Smith, their most experienced performer, directing operations from the middle . . . the free-running of Roger Smart and Peter Noble, the power of the two Dons, Heath and Rogers.

Mention Swindon anywhere and Don Rogers' name follows as some reflex action. Town have long leaned on his striking power. He has a broad commission in attack which lets him free to slip into what he sees as the most advantageous positions. The many goals he has scored prove how effectively he does this.

This power is much more in evidence on his own County Ground than when Town travel. His contribution, in fact, in clearing those last few hurdles before this Final was not particularly inspiring.

But on the spacious Wembley pitch his speed and venomous shooting could be Arsenal's biggest worry.

Remember, however, that Rogers, and Swindon, have to crack the finest defence in the League, to come through. They have to shatter the poise and discipline,

FRANK McLINTOCK . . . his time is coming

SCORERS AND CROWDS

Second Round			
Arsenal (Neill)	1	Sunderland 0	28,460
Third Round			
Scunthorpe (Simpson o.g.)	1	Arsenal 6 (Jenkins 3, Sammels, Gould, Court)	17,450
Fourth Round			
Arsenal (Simpson, Radford)	2	Liverpool 1 (Lawler)	39,299
Fifth Round			
Arsenal (Armstrong 2, Radford, Gould, Simpson)	5	Blackpool 1 (Green)	32,321
SEMI-FINAL			
Arsenal (Radford)	1	Tottenham 0	55,237
Tottenham (Greaves)	1	Arsenal 1 (Radford)	55,925
First Round			
Swindon (Smart, Noble)	2	Torquay 1 (Rowlands)	14,702
Second Round			
Bradford C. (Leighton)	1	Swindon 1 (Smart)	7,806
Swindon (Smith, Rogers, Noble, Stowell o.g.)	4	Bradford C. 3 (Middleton, Hall, Ham)	12,214
Third Round			
Swindon (Rogers)	1	Blackburn 0	15,402
Fourth Round			
Coventry (Tudor, Hateley)	2	Swindon 2 (Rogers, Smart)	23,588
Swindon (Rogers, Smart, Penman)	3	Coventry 0	23,828
Fifth Round			
Derby	0	Swindon 0	35,000
Swindon (Rogers)	1	Derby 0	26,449
SEMI-FINAL			
Burnley (Coates)	1	Swindon 2 (Harland, Noble)	26,231
Swindon (Smith)	1	Burnley 2 (Casper, Kindon)	28,000
PLAY-OFF*			
Swindon (Smith, Bellamy o.g., Noble)	3	Burnley 2 (Thomas, Casper)	20,000

* At the Hawthorns, West Bromwich.

▲ March 1969

THIS TIME···

the telepathic understanding of Storey, Ure, Simpson and McNab AFTER they break through, if they can, the earlier barrier which Sammels, Court and McLintock throw up.

If Swindon succeed where most First Division forward lines have fallen back, blunted then broken, theirs would be the giant-killing act of the last decade.

Third Division Queen's Park Rangers, we know, came from behind two years ago to shock West Bromich Albion in a Final which really gave the League Cup— being decided for the first time at Wembley—a sure grip on a Soccer public still to be wholly won over to it.

But the gap in class is much wider this time.

Rangers then were surely a good cut or two above the present Town side—their continuing success proved it, and the West Bromwich of 1967 did not match up to today's Gunners—*so Rangers did not have to find as much extra as Swindon will need to do to ram these lines back in my teeth.*

Armstrong, Gould, Radford, Graham, whichever the Arsenal front runners, won't be given the freedom of Wembley by any means.

But with eight of last year's losing side to try again, the taste of occasion, the spur of going one better this time, above all, their belief in themselves as a proven good team, IT WILL BE ARSENAL'S LEAGUE CUP.

PAST WINNERS
1960-61 Aston Villa beat Rotherham (agg. 3-2)
1961-62 Norwich City beat Rochdale (agg. 4-0)
1962-63 Birmingham City beat Aston Villa (agg. 3-1)
1963-64 Leicester City beat Stoke City (agg. 4-3)
1964-65 Chelsea beat Leicester City (agg. 3-2)
1965-66 West Bromwich beat West Ham (agg. 5-3)
1966-67 Queen's Park Rangers 3, West Bromwich 2
1967-68 Leeds U. I, Arsenal 0

JOHN SMITH (right) in action . . . Swindon's most experienced performer

How do you tell a 5-year-old that your world is shattered?

ARSENAL SKIPPER FRANK McLINTOCK RELIVES

WHEN I got home from Wembley on Saturday evening after the Football League Cup Final, the first to greet me was my five-year old son Neil. "*Daddy, daddy, where's the Cup,*" he asked as soon as I got through the door.

How do you answer a question like that? How do you explain to a five-year-old that the bottom had just dropped out of your world. That you had been to Wembley for the fourth time, and still come home a loser? Perhaps I should have been used to being second after four attempts. But this was the biggest shock of all. This time, I and my Arsenal team-mates had been so confident that we would bring a new trophy back to Highbury. But Third Division Swindon shattered that ambition . . . and my attempt to break a Wembley hoodoo.

To lose once or twice at Wembley is heartbreaking enough . . . but four times! I felt as if a nightmare had come true.

Four times I've made that slow agonizing walk back to the dressing rooms while the reporters and photographers rushed to acclaim the winners. In a delirium of noise and madness you slip off the pitch dejected and unnoticed, with a tankard or medal as consolation clutched in one hand . . . a poor substitute for the Cup!

Defeat by a Third Division side was hard to take. I couldn't believe that I had finished a loser again. After collecting my tankard from Princess Margaret I just kept walking. I would wake up from a bad dream any moment, I thought. The banging of drums and clash of cymbals soon brought me down to earth—I had wandered among the band—so engrossed was I with

The pleasure (?) of an Army escort, but for McLintock—gloom. Going off after defeat by Swindon—his fourth defeat at Wembley

THE AGONY OF HIS FOURTH LOSING WEMBLEY

disappointment! We were confident before the match—what First Division side facing a team from a lower division wouldn't be?—but we didn't take our chances and Swindon did . . . it was as simple as that!

The man who really broke our hearts was Swindon 'keeper Peter Downsborough who turned in the performance of a lifetime to beat off our continual second-half bombardment on his goal. He made miraculous saves from Jon Sammels and Bob McNab. We wondered if we would ever beat him.

It's terrible to lose to a Third Division side. Wembley's worst-

ever pitch and our fading stamina due to the after effects of a 'flu epidemic won't be considered in the record-books . . . only that stunning score-line.

Before each of my Finals I've asked myself—will this be MY turn? Instead, I've stood back and watched with envy as Danny Blanchflower, Noel Cantwell, Billy Bremner and then Stan Harland climbed the steps to the Royal Box to receive either the F.A. or League Cup.

To lose at Wembley before 100,000 spectators and millions more on television is a sickening experience.

It's like a court trial . . . heroes if you win . . . but condemned as fail-

ures if you lose. That failure tag has hung around my neck four times. You've let down the directors, coach, manager, fans—everybody connected with the club.

The Wembley dressing-room becomes a morgue. Players are too choked too speak. The cheering for the winners still rings in your ears . . . and it's then you realise you are second best.

On the Sunday after the final I could not get the defeat out of my mind. I read the papers over and over again, then looked at the game on television . . . it felt like having a tooth out. My family shared my disappointment; for their sakes I had

Daddy, daddy, where's the Cup...?

longed to get home from Wembley happy ... for once.

That Wembley hoodoo began back in 1961 in the F.A. Cup Final with Spurs, when I was with Leicester. Defeat didn't feel quite so bad the first time. I found it a thrilling experience just to play at Wembley.

We surprised many people that day with the quality of our football and I believe we could have won if Len Chalmers our right-back had not been carried off injured after only 15 minutes. But, a grand reception was held afterwards ... at the Dorchester Hotel and defeat was soon forgotten.

Leicester reached the Final two years later against Manchester United. We had been in the running for the double that season but lost our six remaining League games—and our chance for the League Championship. The side never recovered for the Final in which Denis Law and Pat Crerand played brilliantly. For the second time in four years I finished a loser.

I became unsettled at Filbert Street, feeling that a change would benefit my game. But I still struggled to find my form after moving to Arsenal in 1964. The £80,000 I had cost the club worried me ... I knew I was not giving them value for it. In a side not playing too well I made little impact.

Eventually, I settled in and then, after 16 years in the wilderness, the Gunners reached Wembley in the League Cup Final of 1968, against Leeds United.

We were determined to win to prove that Arsenal had become a real force again, even though Leeds were made clear favourites. But my jinx struck again. We lost a disappointing game by that goal scored by Terry Cooper. So for the third time I was a runner-up. And if anybody had been able to tell me then that it was to happen to me again a year later I think I would have dug a big hole and crawled into it!

But with that sort of luck you have to look to a brighter side. Right now I am determined that FIFTH time is going to be lucky for me. And my consolation is that I HAVE been to Wembley four times ... many a player goes through his career without once experiencing the thrill of a Wembley Final.

As with everything else, in football the show must go on and the next game you play is the important one.

What had seemed then to be the end of the world is now the start toward another goal for Arsenal. We will be back fighting for the honours again.

Leeds United came through after the same sort of set-backs we at Highbury have had. It was an achievement to get to Wembley last March and one defeat cannot take it all away from us.

Arsenal had a good season. At one time, we were bidding strongly for all three honours—the League title, F.A. Cup and the League Cup.

And here I must pay tribute to the man who has worked so hard with the Arsenal players to bring about a great improvement.

I mean our coach and now assistant-manager, Don Howe. He has handsomely filled the gap left when Dave Sexton went to Chelsea ... and we Arsenal players thought that would be a big thing for anybody to do.

With the great team-spirit at Highbury, and the ambition all round, our day will come—and soon.

For it is my ambition to go home one future Saturday evening to young Neil and hand him a cup ... before he even asks!

Gordon Banks jumps high to thwart the menacing Denis Law. Richie Norman and Frank McLintock are in attendance in the Cup Final of 1963.

CONFIDENCE!

...that's what Arsenal's given me, says BOBBY GOULD

PLENTY of people ask me what I think football's all about, and there's only one answer I could ever give—CONFIDENCE. That's what you need, by the bucketful, and I'll tell you straight that confidence is something I've really acquired only in full measure this last year.

I didn't always have much of it in my days at Coventry. Certainly I was well short of it when I came down to Arsenal, but the main reason for that was the £90,000 fee they paid for me—it was a real millstone round my neck for a time, though I'll admit I had no complaints about my share of it!

Seriously, when a club have paid that much for you it's a bit of a worry trying to live up to the label—until you realise, as I did, that it's not really your job to worry about the transfer fee—after all, I didn't pay it.

But last season I think I—and the Gunners, of course—made great strides. And I feel that this year we're really going to win something at last. It's all very well finishing high in the League and reaching the League Cup Final, but we didn't win any medals and those are the things that count.

Y'know, talking about Cup Finals and winning the League bring me up with a jolt. Why? Well not so long ago—eight years to be exact, when I was 15—I walked out of Coventry's ground thinking my football career was all over before it had really started.

It happened like this. The very night I left school in Coventry—my home town —I went over to Birmingham and had a trial with City. They said they'd let me know, but the next day I was at Highfield Road for a trial with the Sky Blues. That went all right, and they gave me a two-month's trial.

Well, at the end of it Billy Frith, then Coventry's manager, called me in and said: "Son, I don't think you'll ever make the grade as a professional—I should go and look for a job!"

You can imagine that was a choker, but anyway I went off and joined a firm of heating engineers. I was all set to start an apprenticeship, too, when Aston Villa gave me a trial on the strength of my performances with a junior side called St. James's. By this time Jimmy Hill had taken over as Coventry manager, he offered me a trial and, hey presto! I was on the groundstaff. Talk about second time lucky!

At 17 I made my first-team debut—that was against Shrewsbury in the Third Division—and that year Coventry were promoted.

You all know what a rapid rise to the top Coventry had, but apart from what he did for the club as a whole, I've no hesitation in naming Jimmy Hill as the man who did most for me. Apart from giving me that wonderful chance, he always seemed to be around—helping, encouraging—everything a young player needed. He threw me in at the deep end and it worked.

Then, of course, we got into the First Division and I had a good start by scoring eight goals early on in the first season up. But then—bang! I came straight back down to earth when I got ligament trouble.

And here's where I have to give a big thank-you to my old pal George Curtis, the Coventry centre-half and a real iron man and a great guy.

George had broken a leg a couple of weeks before—we were having a bad time with injuries then—and it was George who encouraged me and kept my spirit up while I was recovering, even though he had enough to worry about.

When I was fit again I came back in a League game against Burnley and scored a hat-trick. That did me a power of good, I can tell you, but it wasn't long before I hit a bad patch. Nothing would go right and I was pretty fed up.

Well, I was saying earlier about the ups and downs of football, and here's the perfect example. Bertie Mee, the Arsenal manager, had been at that Burnley game and while I was having this bad spell he made a bid for me. There wasn't a more surprised player in England than me at the time.

Anyway, it was all over in a flash and I was packing my boots for London. My wife Marjorie was looking just as dazed as me and thinking the same thing—a couple of years before this was just a dream, now here we were on the way.

Even that £90,000 label and even the thoughts that were flashing through my mind—would I be a failure? Would I fit in at Highbury?—even all that couldn't stop me feeling excited at the prospect of joining a club with a great name like Arsenal.

And I'm glad I did. They've been wonderful to me—the rest of the lads, the manager, coach Don Howe—all of them made me feel at home. In fact, I even enjoy training these days, because it's given such a lot of variety and therefore interest at Highbury that it's not the old-fashioned slog it used to be.

Let's face it—and this is something any youngster should bear in mind—playing football for a living is more training than anything else, so you might as well like it than lump it.

Anyway, whatever happens this season, you won't see us going under for lack of fitness or effort. The rest of the First Division had better take this as a warning—we're a good side, this year we'll prove it by picking up a cup or two. SO WATCH OUT!

▲ September 1969

South Africa...West Indies...Malta ...Italy...Greece...West Germany

HAVE BOOTS-

says JON SAMMELS of Arsenal

I know that it has been said often enough before, but I make no apologies for taking the line that any professional sportsman is among the favoured ones of this world. For where else can one expect to be well paid for doing something that one enjoys?

Still a young man—I have been with Arsenal for nine years and in addition to being kept in top physical shape and playing the game I love, I have been able to travel far more extensively than have most people of my age!

There have been my Under-23 international appearances, and I have toured with Arsenal in South Africa, the West Indies, Malta, Cyprus, Turkey, Hungary, Italy, Greece, West Germany, Holland, Switzerland, France and Bulgaria!

And as these tours have been in the close season, we have usually enjoyed good weather. Perhaps the most enjoyable tour was that to South Africa where the weather was great, and the opposition though keen and anxious to learn, was not really in our class.

They tried hard enough, but we were able to win all five games of the tour without really extending ourselves. We had a good time, too, in Cyprus with its lovely climate and smashing beaches. *I could take a lot of that!*

Mind you, we've had our dubious moments too! I will never forget one game in Turkey v. Fenerbahce, in Ankara, under floodlights. We had been playing for about thirty minutes when suddenly—out went the lights, leaving the whole stadium in complete darkness!

We stood in groups in the middle of the pitch waiting for something to happen. I almost expected a huge Turk to appear brandishing a curved sword!! I stood alongside the big boys that time!

But all was well, for eventually the lights came on again and the game proceeded. It is trips and instances such as this that make this game of ours what it is —*the greatest*!

But, of course, the guts of British Soccer are our domestic, League and F.A. Cup competitions, and my own entry into the game is typical of the manner in which League clubs scour the country to make certain that potential players of the future, get their opportunity.

I was born in Ipswich and due to my dad serving in the R.A.F., I attended several schools in my youth as he was posted to various stations, but most of my schoolboy Soccer was played at Grundisburgh Primary School, and from the age of 11 at Farlingaye Secondary Modern—both near Ipswich.

And in my early teens I had my first taste of representative Soccer when I played for Suffolk County Schoolboys.

When I was 15, apparently having been noticed by an Arsenal scout, I was invited for a trial to the club's training centre at London Colney. I could have signed apprentice forms then, but it was decided that I should stay at school for a further term, and I actually signed (for Mr. George Swindin who was then the manager) just short of 16.

I had always played inside-forward and I signed in January. For the rest of that season I was in this position in the Youth and "A" teams, making my debut in the reserves the next term—my first full season with the Highbury club.

My first-team debut was in a League game v. Blackpool at Bloomfield Road where, although we lost 2-3 after scoring in the first minute, I notched our second— my first League goal for the club.

Which brings me back with a jolt to our defeat by the same margin in this season's third round F.A. Cup replay on the same ground.

Again, we took an early lead when it fell to me to open the scoring with a 20-yarder. John Radford put us two-up before the interval, but Blackpool came back in the second half to grab the winner—and passage into round four—in injury time.

It was a dreadful disappointment for, having taken the lead, we were very much top-dogs and this carried on after the interval—until after bringing on their substitute on the hour, Blackpool suddenly found a reserve of power.

But that's football—it has its sad and great moments. I am thinking of our two defeats in the Football League Cup Finals at Wembley. The first of these (the 1-0 defeat by Leeds United) was a tactical triumph for the Yorkshire side, but our 3-1 beating by Swindon Town last season was tragedy.

We were losing 1-0 when Bobby Gould equalised. Shortly before I had let fly with a first-time volley from outside the penalty box (from where I seem to score most of what goals come my way) and the Swindon 'keeper Peter Downsborough made a brilliant save to push the ball round the post.

Had that one gone in (and goodness knows it should have done!) we would have won. As it was, extra time

▲ March 1970

...Cyprus...Turkey...Hungary
...Holland...Switzerland...France

WILL TRAVEL

brought two great goals from Don Rogers —and we were out in the cold again.

Without wishing to detract in any way from the (then) Third Division side, on reflection the heavy state of the Wembley pitch (notorious at that time) had a far more weakening effect on us, than it had on Swindon. Eight of our lads had been down with 'flu, and the extra time necessary, took its toll.

On the brighter side—one of the most satisfying of Arsenal's games in recent seasons was when in 1967-68 we licked our traditional North London enemies Spurs 4-0 at Highbury. It just so happened that all our lads chose this game as the

one to hit their top form, and we demoralised our neighbours, making ourselves and our supporters feel very good, indeed.

On a more personal note, possibly my brightest memory is of a game at Highbury against a Brazilian XI when we won 2-0—and I scored both.

Mine is usually a midfield job, hence I do not get a lot of goals, but—as I mentioned above—my goals came from my favourite position, outside the penalty area.

Don't ask me why. What I do know is that when we are on the attack, I am usually operating just behind the strikers and if I see an opening, I let go.

I wish it could happen more often!

FOOTBALL MONTHLY

PETER STOREY
Arsenal

CYRIL KNOWLES
Spurs

COCK-A-HOOP!

Skipper Frank McLintock proudly displays the European Fairs Cup to enthusiastic fans outside Islington Town Hall where they received a civic reception in honour of their victory. Below: Arsenal players and officials in their open-topped bus.

Arsenal
FOOTBALL CLUB

◄ May 1969 | 1970–71 Gift Book ▲

It took a trip behind the Iron Curtain to show me what the name of Arsenal means in World Soccer

I WAS BORN WITH RED-AND-WHITE EYES!

BY CHARLIE GEORGE

HAVE you ever had a dream that was about to come true—then had it fall down flat?

That's what happened to me on my League debut against Everton on the opening day of last season.

I had always dreamed of playing for Arsenal—but what I thought would be the biggest moment of my life turned out to be a terrible flop.

I just couldn't get going and to top it all, we lost to a Johnny Hurst goal in the final minutes.

But one person really bucked me up—Everton's skipper and World Cup centre-half Brian Labone. As I was walking off at the finish he came up, put his arm round my shoulders and said: " Forget it son, go out and have a drink, things will get better."

I felt really down in the dumps, and, believe me, those few words helped a lot. What's more, the game taught me a valuable lesson—*don't expect too much, too soon!*

Yet despite what happened on the field, nothing will ever give me a greater thrill than when I slipped on the famous red-and-white jersey for the first time. You see, I reckon I must have been the only kid born with red and white eyes!

I was born only five minutes from Arsenal Stadium. Everything took second place to watching the Gunners, and I've lost count of the times I got a ticking-off from my parents for travelling anything up to 200 miles to see an away game!

So you can imagine how I felt as I lined up with players like Frank McLintock and Terry Neill. Though the game might have turned out better I learned an awful lot about first-grade football.

Everything was so much tougher and faster than I'd been used to. In all honesty, it was easy for me to be out-standing as a schoolboy . . . but in the First Division you only have to lose concentration for a split second and you're left trailing.

What's more the atmosphere and pressures are enough to send chills running down the spines of established players let along a raw kid of 18! You almost feel frightened of letting anybody down.

I think the turning point for me came in a League match against West Bromwich Albion at the Hawthorns.

If I was depressed after the Everton game, then I felt ten feet tall at the Hawthorns!

Apart from scoring my first League goal, it was also the only one of the game and Arsenal's first of the season!

John Radford centred a low ball, Jimmy Robertson jumped over it and I fired home between Albion players Doug Fraser and John Talbot. What a feeling . . . I wanted to jump over the moon!

Yet the next match—against Leeds at Highbury—was, for me, the highlight of last season.

Imagine me, Charlie George, lining up opposite world-class players like Billy Bremner, Jack Charlton, Norman Hunter, Gary Sprake and Allan Clarke. It was enough to take my breath away.

I was a little overawed at first, but once I settled, I felt I played my best game of last season. The match finished 1–1 and I felt I had really arrived!

I suppose I HAD to become a foot-baller. Soccer runs right through the family.

My uncle Horace Woodward, was a famous Spurs centre-half during the Fifties and later went on to play with Queen's Park Rangers. Another uncle, Freddie George, won an England amateur cap while playing for Finchley.

But for me it was always Arsenal though it took a trip behind the Iron Curtain to Rumania to really bring home to me just what that name means in the Soccer world.

We were drawn against Dinamo Bacau in the Fairs Cup. It just didn't seem possible: 1,563 miles across Europe to a new land and a new way of life . . . for a football match!

The flight to Bucharest took just over three-and-a-half hours and when we touched down the Rumanians gave us the sort of welcome that is usually reserved for royalty!

▲ 1970–71 Gift Book

Above: Charlie rides a tackle from David Payne of Crystal Palace.

Right: In dispute with referee Dennis Turner in a game at Highbury.

Thousands lined the road cheering as we made our way from the airport to our hotel. And as a tribute to Arsenal's visit, the Rumanian Government promptly declared Wednesday—match day—a NATIONAL HOLIDAY!

The journey to Bacau was like a fairy-tale scene with snow-capped mountains shining in the sun and fir trees bending in the breeze.

Everywhere we went the locals seemed to go out of their way to be helpful and friendly. And the way the town responded to the match you would have thought it was the World Cup final. About 20,000 people crammed into the tiny but tidy stadium and the support they gave Bacau was tremendous.

Unfortunately we couldn't repay their hospitality on the pitch. We romped home 2–0 with goals from Jon Sammels and John Radford.

There was an incredible sight at the end. Somebody threw a firecracker that set alight a piece of turf! I reckon they must have been trying to turn Peter Marinello and me into skinheads!

That trip was certainly an experience I won't forget in a hurry.

Another marvellous occasion was our victory over Anderlecht in the Fairs Cup Final last season . . . Arsenal's first major success for 17 years.

And what a moment for me . . . in my first full season . . . landing a winners' medal.

The scenes after our second-leg victory at Highbury were fantastic. The players were throwing jerseys, shorts, everything out of the Arsenal dressing-room to delirious fans in the street. Champagne was spilling everywhere!

Mind you, things didn't always go so well last season. Especially the night I was sent off playing against Irish part-timers Glentoran in another Fairs Cup-tie.

A linesman's decision went against me and in the heat of the moment I very stupidly told him what I thought of him . . . only to find myself walking to the dressing-room!

I felt sick. I had let down everybody and afterwards I was severely reprimanded by manager Bertie Mee. That was another lesson learned: *Keep your mouth shut!*

What really set me on the path to professional football was the Soccer set-up at my school at Holloway, North London. It was so well organised that I kept on improving.

Guess who helped coach me? . . . Bob Wilson—now my team-mate at Highbury. Bob used to coach us on his spare after-noons along with Mike England, of Spurs, and Trevor Hartley, then of West Ham and now down at Bourne-mouth.

Now I can't stop Bob from saying that I owe my success to his wonderful coaching! But seriously, Bob is an extremely good coach and I learned a great deal from him.

But the person to whom I owe most is Steve Burtenshaw, Arsenal's second string coach. He gave me endless advice and encouragement and what's more he drummed into me that a player can have all the natural talent in the world but he won't get anywhere unless he is prepared to work and work.

LIFE'S SWEET FOR 'SUGAR RAY' KENNEDY

SIR STANLEY Matthews beckoned the big, shy-looking lad into his office at Port Vale and said: "Sorry son, you're not going to make it . . . you're not fast enough."

That's how Soccer's first Knight once threw Arsenal's new shooting star, Ray Kennedy, on to the scrapheap.

Convinced he had no future in professional football, a dejected Kennedy returned home to Seaton Delaval in Whitley Bay, Northumberland, and found a job as a sugar boiler in a sweet factory.

That was just over two years ago . . . but now his rejection rates nothing more than just a bad dream.

The fact that Kennedy was able to withstand such a body-blow from a legendary figure like Matthews and still come back, is a triumph of character and determination.

Kennedy has rocketed to fame this season, his opportunist goals making him one of the hottest properties on the Highbury books.

He topped the list of First Division marksmen after only a handful of first-team appear-

Kennedy challenged by ex-Gunner Ian Ure of Manchester United at Highbury

ances and earned Young England recognition from Sir Alf Ramsey for the international against West Germany at Leicester in October.

How is it that kid Kennedy should hit it off with championship chasing Arsenal after being discarded at Fourth Division Vale Park?

He says: "I spent a year on the Vale groundstaff and most of my time was taken up with general duties like cleaning boots and sweeping the terraces. That's fair enough, as these sort of duties must be accepted at a club with limited finances.

"But what I couldn't understand was that I got very little Soccer coaching and had to train in my spare time. At Arsenal everything is geared to helping players develop their basic skills and tactical appreciation.

"Stan's a wonderful bloke really, but I think he saw me wrong. He was looking for ball-play and speed and that's just not my game. I do lack pace but through intensive coaching I feel I've developed other assets to compensate this weakness.

"For example, I am now reading a game better and arriving in better positions to receive the ball."

Kennedy's experience with the Potteries club makes one wonder how many other youngsters have been cast aside by clubs unable to bring out the best in them.

Kennedy, 5 ft. 11 in. and 13½ stone, yet still only 19, was originally spotted playing for South Northumberland Boys by Bill Emery—a civil servant and part-time scout who lives in North Shields. It was on Emery's recommendation that Kennedy went to Port Vale.

After his rebuff there Kennedy played for New Hartley Juniors, banging in goals galore and continuing to grow.

Then came Don Emerson . . .

Emerson, a full-time scout in the North-East, was sufficiently impressed with Kennedy to send him down to London for a trial with Arsenal.

Says Kennedy: "One night there was a knock on the door

▲ February 1971

FOOTBALL
MONTHLY

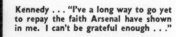

and my brother answered it. It was Emerson.

"I couldn't believe it. I get thrown out at Port Vale, then I find that Arsenal want me. You'd think it was someone playing some kind of sick joke.

"Anyway, I spent four days at Highbury and it was great. I settled in right away."

Kennedy served his apprenticeship, spent last season gaining experience in the reserves, then gratefully grabbed a regular first-team spot this season after Charlie George was injured in the opening League fixture at Everton. And it's been goals all the way.

Listen to what coach Don Howe has to say about his exciting young prospect: "Ray has it in him to go to the top. He was told, like many apprentices, that he wasn't good enough. So he went all out to prove them wrong and has done it in a higher class.

"We always felt Ray would do well. For a big boy he is quite quick and skilful. He was 18 months behind the other lads but he soon caught up because he is a willing worker.

"A lot of the credit must go to reserve team coach Steve Burtenshaw. He has given him a lot of confidence. He spent afternoon after afternoon helping him.

"John Radford has also had a lot to do with Ray's success, advising him on and off the field. They have now struck up a great understanding."

Kennedy gave a sample of what was to come last season in Brussels in the first leg of the Gunners' Fairs Cup Final against the Belgian side, Anderlecht.

With only 12 minutes left and Arsenal 3-0 down, Charlie George limped off and was replaced by Kennedy. For his first touch of the ball he soared above the Anderlecht defence to head home a George Armstrong cross.

The goal was a tremendous boost for Arsenal's dented morale and they swept home to glory in the return at Highbury to end 17 barren years without a major trophy.

Kennedy, reserved and courteous, does not delude himself about the future: "It would be easy for me to sit back and think success will just happen. But I've got a long way to go yet to repay the faith Arsenal have shown in me. I can't be grateful enough for the confidence everyone at Highbury have given me."

Esso stations are giving away
FREE FOOTBALL CLUB BADGES

Fantastic good news for football fans! Esso stations are giving away–yes giving away–76 beautiful full-colour badge replicas of all leading clubs in the League. And what a dazzling collection they make! Every one has a shiny metal finish and is embossed and printed in the club colours. You get a FREE COLLECTOR CARD, too–with spaces to stick in your badges and lots of details about each club. And it's all absolutely free!

Just ask the Esso forecourt man for your free badges and free collector card when you drive in at the special Esso sign.

2 FREE BADGES
when you drive in at this sign.

Special 'Starter Pack' of 26 Badges–only 20p.

Get your collection off to a flying start with this special pack of 26 football club badges.

 **The Action Station.**

▲ October 1971

**FRANK
McLINTOCK**
Arsenal

▲ April 1971

May 1971 ▶▶

Frank Clarke (Ipswich), out for goals, bumped into Bob Wilson

Irate Arsenal players surrounded Clarke demanding to know

in agony. But all was well after the trainer had been on to see to

FOOTBALL MONTHLY

Arsenal), out to stop him...and Bob was hurt in trying to do so.

what he thought he was up to as their goalkeeper rolled about

Wilson.

Clarke (9) begins his run. McNeil seen next bending over Wilson. Clarke has gone on, then Arsenal players confront him. Trainer George Wright arrives and Robertson (Ipswich) sympathetically joins his ex-colleagues.

DETERMINATION

**Determination . . .
as Storey shields
the ball from
Leicester's Len
Glover**

PETER STOREY'S iron resolution and all-round talents made a massive contribution to the cause of Arsenal this last season . . . talents which received belated public recognition.

If you used just one word to describe his game it would be DETERMINATION. The sort of gritty determination that has turned an England-class fullback into one of the best midfield men in the business; the steely dedication that can turn a cheerful character off the field into a cold-eyed enemy on it.

Such intense determination was perfectly illustrated in that epic F.A. Cup semi-final at Hillsborough when Arsenal were awarded a last-minute penalty against Stoke City.

The agonising face-to-face confrontation between ice-man Storey and England ace Gordon Banks is unlikely to be equalled for dramatic impact for as long as 55,000 partisan witnesses will remember.

As Storey, outwardly resigned but inwardly restive, stepped up to beat Banks with his dramatic spot-kick, a huge cheer signalled relief and released Arsenal's all-action midfield man from a responsibility that few would have envied and fewer still accepted.

As Arsenal manager Bertie Mee admitted: "At a moment like that I couldn't think of a player I would have rather trusted with the task."

Skipper Frank McLintock echoed the admiration of his boss when he said: "Peter was on a hiding to nothing and I would have forgiven him if he had asked to be spared this ordeal.

"But no, that's not like Peter Storey. He stepped straight up and ended the unbearable tension by slotting home the equaliser.

"It was agony for the rest of us, and I dread to think what it must have been for Peter. But he just accepted the situation."

Storey himself admitted: "Yes, it was quite a moment. As soon as Mahoney handled the ball and the ref pointed to the spot, the lads went potty. Some were leaping and shouting 'We've saved it.'

"It was all right for them. I still had to stick it in. I knew I would be either a hero or a mug so there was only one way

to settle it. I ambled up and belted it. But it seemed to take three hours to go into that net!"

Arsenal manager Bertie Mee once described Peter as the perfect professional. No one who was at Hillsborough that day will ever argue about that.

He has also been described by some as a "hard nut." No one who has ever come out of a 50-50 tackle with Storey will deny that either.

Yet to think of Storey as merely a hard man is to dismiss his many talents and his undoubted temperament for the big occasion.

Colleague George Armstrong quickly dismisses the suggestion that his team-mate is just "a hard man", whose only contribution to the side is in his tackling.

Says George: "Peter is a very underestimated player. He's a bloke who gets on with his job because he relishes it. He has made a great success of his midfield role this season because he is utterly determined not to let anyone down. In the process he has proved that he is quite a footballer.

"He's got quite a bit more skill than people give him credit for. He played a blinder at Hillsborough and did us proud when he took that penalty with so much at stake.

"Peter's ice-cool in a crisis. He's got nerves of steel. No one wants to take a penalty in the dying seconds of a game—especially a Cup semi-final when you're 2-1 down. But Peter kept his head and slotted it away."

What of the accusations that Storey is just a hard man who sorts people out?

"Utterly stupid," insists Armstrong. "Peter's tackling, and his timing of a tackle, have always been superb. He's hard, but he's definitely not vicious.

"He's not in the team just to sort people out, but he is a very good marker—as George Best will testify. He's good because he gives every job 100 per cent-plus.

"But he doesn't hold grudges or make threats. He can look after himself on the field, but he doesn't cry when he gets a knock —and he gets plenty. Peter accepts this like a true professional.

"I can tell you that he gets more than his share of them. That's because he's fearless. He doesn't wear pads and he doesn't pull out of tackles because he is a 100 per center.

"Off the field he is a bit quiet. You don't get much out of him. But he's got a very keen sense of humour and lets himself go a bit after a game.

▲ June 1971

FLAIR = PETER STOREY

"Perhaps his greatest asset is his tremendous enthusiasm for the game. It even shows out in training. He gives it everything he's got; just as he does when he is out there on the field for Arsenal.

"He really deserved his call-up to the England squad for his great displays last season. One thing you can be sure of: he will never let England down . . . no matter where they play him."

England colleague Bob McNab, Peter's closest friend at Highbury, also pays unstinted tribute to the performances of super-man Storey this season.

Says Bob: "I used to think he was a great full-back. No-one ever got past him, and I'll never know why he didn't win an England Under-23 cap in that position.

"He went into midfield originally to win the ball. But now he's doing a lot more than that for us. His accuracy in passing and his non-stop enthusiasm has given us that something extra in midfield.

"Sure, Peter's a bit of a hard man, and anyone who complains about his style of play, to my mind, is not criticising him as much as complimenting his effectiveness.

"And what about the goals

George Armstrong . . . "Peter doesn't hold grudges or make threats"

he's scored? Most of them have been pressure goals and have again proved that Peter has the ideal temperament to make a success of his new job."

Yes, the continuing progress of Peter Storey is one of the main reasons why Arsenal have done so well this past two seasons.

His drive and dedication is now an integral part of the side, just as the fiery leadership of Billy Bremner has added a new dimension to Leeds United's rise in the past few years.

Players like Bremner and Storey have had to break down a few barriers to be accepted in the fullest football sense.

They are loved and hated, depending on which side you support. But they are never, never left out of the side.

Peter Storey is winning himself a lot more fans for the flair and skills that he has added to his game.

But the game will always be the same for Storey himself. Ninety minutes of all-out effort.

RAY BRADLEY

Ice-cool Storey beats Banks to earn a semi-final replay

SALUTE TO ARSENAL

White Hart Lane . . .
Where Kennedy's header had
clinched the League Championship

	Home						Away						
	P	W	D	L	F	A	W	D	L	F	A	Pts
Leeds	35	13	2	2	32	10	10	6	2	28	17	54
Arsenal	32	13	3	0	35	6	8	3	5	22	19	48
Chelsea	35	10	5	2	30	18	6	7	5	17	18	44
Wolves	34	11	2	4	28	21	7	5	5	27	28	43
Southmptn	34	11	5	1	27	8	3	6	8	17	27	39
Tottenhm	32	8	4	4	26	16	6	6	4	19	14	38
Liverpool												

First Division—five weeks to go . . .

UP THE

IT ALL CAME RIGHT in the end, but if and when another club comes up with the League and Cup double which Bertie Mee's boys have laid before their frenetic fans it is to be hoped for the sake of Soccer sanity that they do so in less exciting, less exhausting fashion than Arsenal, 1970-71.

It is good and healthy for them to have at long last stuffed all the legends of the Thirties and what-they-did-in-Chapman's days deep down in the waste paper basket.

It is good to see this always big club now able to hold eye-to-eye level talks with those draped with the success of recent years . two League Cup Finals, a Fairs Cup triumph then this capture of the Big Two . . . they are again walking knee-deep in honours.

Remember this about the winning of the double for the fourth time . . . that Leeds United remained the favourites to win the

League Championship when the Gunners had to go to White Hart Lane for the last night of reckoning. And that Liverpool were the favourites when the teams lined up to meet the Duke of Kent on Final day at Wembley.

Some chance they were given —whoever heard of the wizards of odds putting their hearts first where they knew the money should be instead?

Take a look at our table here. The one you will know well is that for the final round-up, with Arsenal a point to the good over Leeds and the pair of 'em almost in a league of their own indicated by the 12-point gap before you get to Spurs and Wolves. This earlier one, *now that tells its own story.*

That table tells the story with some five weeks to go and it is the story on FA Cup semi-finals day. While Arsenal were hanging on by their bootlaces to their Cup interest, with Peter Storey clipping a penalty past Gordon Banks in the last minute for a

2-2 draw, Chelsea were doin Arsenal a great favour with blinding 3-1 League win ov Leeds and form which Stamfo Bridge regulars had been waiti all season to see.

There it was then . . . Arsen had to battle it out with Sto again, this time at Villa Park the following Wednesday, we six points down on Leeds wi three more games extra to pla in the 10 needed to comple their fixtures.

This is where any other writ would have been telling you th no author of schoolboy fictie would have dared to dream up plot on the lines of what actual did take place!

In exactly a month they ha ten League matches to play, rate of two a week. Had to t to march step by step with Lee who already had the points . and still try to budget for Live pool in the Final, to which the had won their way after easi disposing of Stoke in that r played semi-final.

It would be enough to tell th

▲ July 1971

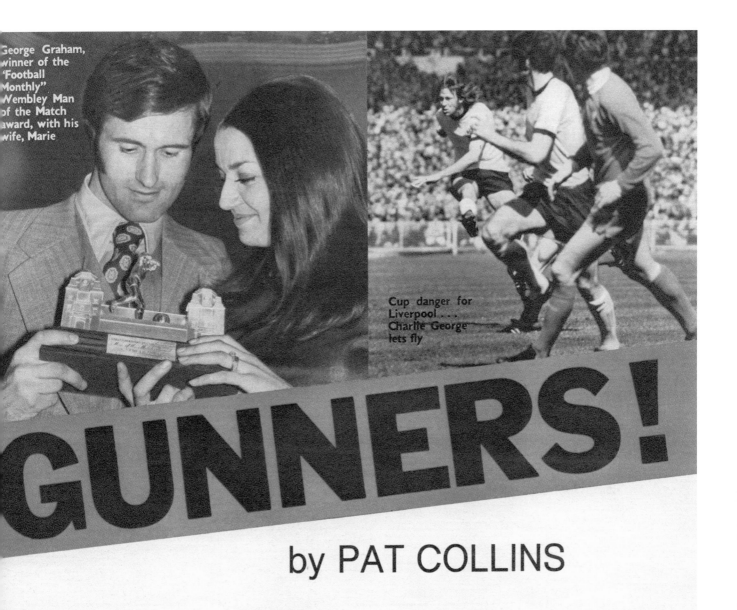

George Graham, winner of the "Football Monthly" Wembley Man of the Match award, with his wife, Marie

Cup danger for Liverpool . . . Charlie George lets fly

GUNNERS!

by PAT COLLINS

Their great surge towards that record-breaking eighth League title win brought them a crop of 23 points from the last 26 they contested so hardily. But that would be missing out on the meat and bones of their stirring story.

Let's get back to that last handful of matches to decide the League crown . . .

Chelsea, usually a stumbling block for Arsenal, Coventry, Southampton, Forest, Newcastle and Burnley were seen off. On that mid-April afternoon when Charlie George moved to the edge of the box to rattle home the lone winner against Newcastle, Leeds were having riot scenes because of a goal which manager Don Revie, his players and crowd swore to a man was never on because of offside against Colin Suggett, of West Brom, before Jeff Astle scored.

That goal cost United two points and cut their advantage, but see how the story unfolded. . .

Arsenal had to go to the Hawthorns a week later, the Albion —they are here again—kept them to just a point while Leeds at The Dell were stepping up the pressure by slamming the Saints . . . prior to meeting the Gunners at Elland Road on the Monday, two days later.

That match was one for the books—and for tranquillisers. Just when Arsenal thought they had gained a trick by taking a point came a scrambled Jack Charlton winner . . . and this time Arsenal flocked round referee Burtenshaw to insist that Leeds had been given an offside goal. And wait . . . HE was the referee they knew would be handling the Final!

Their protests availed them nowt, the goal stood. And very sensibly manager Bertie Mee refused to talk of any Arsenal objection to Mr. B at Wembley. In fact, said he thought that he was "a very good referee."

No script-writer would ever have dared to drop in this meet-

HOW THEY WON THE LEAGUE TITLE

Aug. 15	Everton	A	2-2	George, Graham
Aug. 17	West Ham	A	0-0	
Aug. 22	Man. Utd.	H	4-0	Radford 3, Graham
Aug. 25	Huddersfield	H	1-0	Kennedy
Aug. 29	Chelsea	A	1-2	Kelly
Sept. 1	Leeds	H	0-0	
Sept. 5	Spurs	H	2-0	Armstrong 2
Sept. 12	Burnley	A	2-1	Kennedy, Radford
Sept. 19	West Brom.	H	6-2	Graham 2, Kennedy 2, Armstrong, Cantello o.g.
Sept. 26	Stoke	A	0-5	
Oct. 3	Nott'm. F.	H	4-0	Kennedy 3, Armstrong
Oct. 10	Newcastle	A	1-1	Graham
Oct. 17	Everton	H	4-0	Kennedy 2, Kelly, Storey (pen.)
Oct. 24	Coventry	A	3-1	Kennedy, Radford, Graham
Oct. 31	Derby	H	2-0	Kelly, Radford

Nov. 7	Blackpool	A	1-0	Radford
Nov. 14	Crystal P.	H	1-1	Radford
Nov. 21	Ipswich	A	1-0	Armstrong
Nov. 28	Liverpool	H	2-0	Graham, Radford
Dec. 5	Man. City	A	2-0	Armstrong, Radford
Dec. 12	Wolves	H	2-0	Graham, Radford
Dec. 19	Man. Utd.	A	3-1	McLintock, Graham, Kennedy
Dec. 26	South'ton	H	0-0	
Jan. 9	West Ham	H	2-0	Graham, Kennedy
Jan. 16	Huddersfield	A	1-2	Kennedy
Jan. 30	Liverpool	A	0-2	
Feb. 6	Man. City	H	1-0	Radford
Feb. 20	Ipswich	H	3-2	George, Radford, McLintock
Feb. 27	Derby	A	0-2	
March 2	Wolves	A	3-0	Kennedy 2, Radford
March 13	Crystal P.	A	2-0	Graham, Sammels

March 20	Blackpool	H	1-0	Storey
April 3	Chelsea	H	2-0	Kennedy 2
April 6	Coventry	H	1-0	Kennedy
April 10	South'ton	A	2-1	Radford, McLintock
April 13	Nott'm F.	A	3-0	McLintock, Kennedy, George
April 17	Newcastle	H	1-0	George
April 20	Burnley	H	1-0	George (pen.)
April 24	West Brom.	A	2-2	McLintock, Hartford o.g.
April 26	Leeds	A	0-1	
May 1	Stoke	H	1-0	Kelly
May 3	Spurs	A	1-0	Kennedy

GOALSCORERS: Kennedy 20; Radford 15; Graham 11; Armstrong 6; George 5; McLintock 5; Kelly 4; Storey 2; Sammels 1. Opponents o.g. 2.

UP THE GUNNERS!

Bertie Mee and his "double" triumph

ing of the main contenders for the title at such a stage. And if one had that would have been the fictitious high-spot of the story. How much further the real thing could and did go!

To decide the title Arsenal just scraped home against Stoke, a grim side giving but nothing, just nothing away because they still felt they had won the right to their first Cup Final when Peter Storey's last gasp penalty stopped them . . . Leeds also won that day, Arsenal had one match to play, the slide rules and the decimals came up with the final demand for Frank McLintock and his men . . .

It must be a win or a 0-0 draw at White Hart Lane . . . just that or Leeds, not Arsenal, are the new champions.

Arsenal were one point be-

Bob Wilson jumps for joy

hind with a goal average of 2·413 to Leeds' 2·400. A goalless draw? There had never been such a finish to any of the previous 69 meetings of these great North London rivals.

Tottenham were playing for bonus money for the third place position . . . and defending their proud claim as the only club this century to have achieved the double.

Plus which, Arsenal had won but a single game on their last 11 trips across the four-mile no-man's land which divides them from Spurs.

Somewhere, somehow there might have been a compelling facet which had been overlooked in this final setting to the first leg of the double, but nobody has yet been able to think what it could have been. Have not *dared* to make a suggestion.

For the record, however, the Gunners went in without key man Storey, who had limped out of the Stoke match. Spurs skipper Alan Mullery came back after missing the previous game . . . referee Kevin Howley was having his last game before retirement and the gates were shut with nearly an hour to go.

Of course, it had to be a rip-roaring affair. Naturally there was no let-up from beginning to end. Surprisingly the razor-edge atmosphere still threw up great football, intense as it all was. And we got almost a last-minute winner when Ray Kennedy headed home. And what else would you have expected?

As Mr. Howley said: "What a wonderful way to go out of the game! If somebody had told me I would finish with a match like this it would have sounded like a fairy tale."

So the Final five days later could have been some sort of anti-climax, much as all High-bury and Islington still wanted to crow over that dream double. Could have been—with Liverpool there?

Certainly the game got bogged down quite a bit . . . long rain on that Wembley turf meant that the pull on players' legs was that much stronger—and it showed. But there was Bill Shankly to beat . . . the Kop crowd to try and drown, there was sunshine . . . and there was McLintock, four times a Wembley loser, looking for it to round off a week which would mean a League-winner's medal. "Foot-

baller of the Year" award . . . and a Cup winner's medal.

In keeping with the hard way they had gone about all else, Arsenal, as we now know, had to go to extra time . . . had to come back from behind and so continue their Cup story of playing every game twice over, all save their Third Round tie with non-League Yeovil . . . and even that match saw them go West before they found piled snow on the pitch postponing the match until the mid-week.

Who could have thought that so frustrating day, with everybody fuming over the futility of the Saturday trip, that this was the start of something as big as it eventually turned out?

In turn, before the second leg had been accomplished, I had chairman Denis Hill-Wood and chief scout Gordon Clark assuring me that this was but the start for Arsenal: that they put no

limit on a run which would keep the Gunners right upsides to the most successful of our clubs, aye, and leading the way.

And assistant-manager Don Howe pursued this same theme while still trying to recover from those palpitating last minutes of the Wembley extra time.

They all, along with Bertie Mee, are quite definite about this, these men who have worked so hard to adjust the balance of power in our game and who have now thrown down this gauntlet . . . with the fingers pointing in a northerly direction.

That is the future, as is the club's first venture into the Champions' Cup and their forthcoming test against the greatest sides in Europe. Meantime they have rekindled a lot of memories as they give greater meaning to the battle cry which once challenged all comers . . . "Up The Gunners!"

PATH TO WEMBLEY

THIRD ROUND: Yeovil A 3-0 Radford 2, Kennedy.

FOURTH ROUND: Portsmouth A 1-1 Storey (pen.); Portsmouth H 3-2 George, Simpson, Storey (pen.).

FIFTH ROUND: Man. City A 2-1 George 2.

SIXTH ROUND: Leicester A 0-0; Leicester H 1-0 George.

SEMI-FINAL: Stoke (at Hillsboro) 2-2 Storey 2 (1 pen.); Stoke (at Villa Park) 2-0 Graham, Kennedy.

FINAL: Liverpool (at Wembley) 2-1 Kelly, George.

Despair for Liverpool keeper Ray Clemence (left) at Wembley . . . jubilation for Pat Rice and matchwinner Charlie George (above)

WE ARE THE C-H-A-M-P-I...
....AND THE CUP-HOLDE...

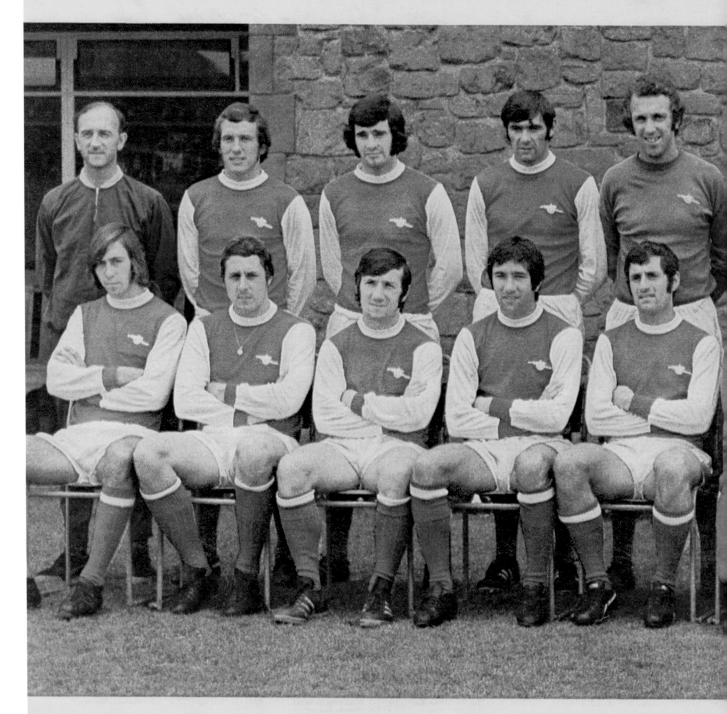

The Arsenal line-up
which made history

▲ July 1971

Standing left to right: George Wright, trainer, Bob McNab, Peter Storey, Peter Simpson, Geoff Barnett, Bob Wilson, John Roberts, Ray Kennedy, Peter Marinello, Don Howe, assistant-manager.
Seated: Charlie George, John Radford, George Armstrong, Jon Sammels, Frank McLintock, Manager Bertie Mee, Pat Rice, Eddie Kelly, George Graham and Sammy Nelson

If she knew you were wearing Levi's she'd lock up her daughter

Mister Levi's. Proper trousers. Neat smart trousers with all the fit, freedom and comfort of Levi's jeans.

So accept her mother's silent approval. Don't admit you feel as relaxed and comfortable as you would in your oldest jeans. She doesn't know that Levi's are now making a whole range of fashionable trousers that look smart. Like the washable knits in the picture.

So don't let on. Act as smart as you look.

▲ April 1972

FOOTBALL
MONTHLY

LY 1971
½p U.S.A. 70 cents

**SALUTE TO ARSENAL:
"UP THE GUNNERS!"**

**SPECIAL: SOCCER
ON THE BREADLINE**

It's a goal all the way!

MAC'S MATCH

There was hardly an echo of last season's tough Cup battles when staff photographer Ian McLellan went to Highbury for Arsenal's League meeting with Leicester City. This time the champions' all-round strength proved too much for the Midlands side and a 3-0 home victory was gained comfortably against struggling rivals

Poor old Leicester, they are on the receiving end of John Radford's power-packed right boot here as we see the Arsenal leader blast off with City's Len Glover in the background. The result is a home goal, first of Radford's two and there he is taking the salute, as it were. And there's no doubt his Arsenal team-mates thought as much about it as their fans . . . for down below we have Peter Storey and John Roberts telling him what a fine job they think he is doing

Whoops! You can understand what made Glover's hair stand on end here. There's plenty of power behind the clearance by Rober and no good would have come of getti in the way

▲ December 1971

Rice is down, but looks to have
barred the way to Partridge as help
arrives in the shape of Roberts

Brown sets off for the far e[...]
but Nelson is in close attendan[...]
jockeying for positi[...]

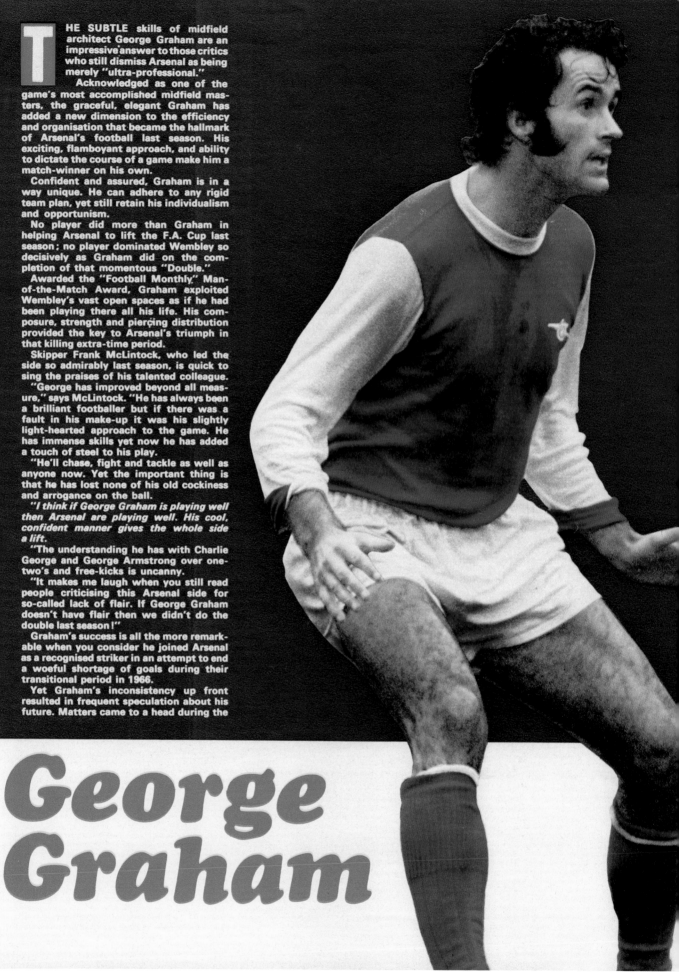

THE SUBTLE skills of midfield architect George Graham are an impressive answer to those critics who still dismiss Arsenal as being merely "ultra-professional."

Acknowledged as one of the game's most accomplished midfield masters, the graceful, elegant Graham has added a new dimension to the efficiency and organisation that became the hallmark of Arsenal's football last season. His exciting, flamboyant approach, and ability to dictate the course of a game make him a match-winner on his own.

Confident and assured, Graham is in a way unique. He can adhere to any rigid team plan, yet still retain his individualism and opportunism.

No player did more than Graham in helping Arsenal to lift the F.A. Cup last season; no player dominated Wembley so decisively as Graham did on the completion of that momentous "Double."

Awarded the "Football Monthly" Man-of-the-Match Award, Graham exploited Wembley's vast open spaces as if he had been playing there all his life. His composure, strength and piercing distribution provided the key to Arsenal's triumph in that killing extra-time period.

Skipper Frank McLintock, who led the side so admirably last season, is quick to sing the praises of his talented colleague.

"George has improved beyond all measure," says McLintock. "He has always been a brilliant footballer but if there was a fault in his make-up it was his slightly light-hearted approach to the game. He has immense skills yet now he has added a touch of steel to his play.

"He'll chase, fight and tackle as well as anyone now. Yet the important thing is that he has lost none of his old cockiness and arrogance on the ball.

"*I think if George Graham is playing well then Arsenal are playing well. His cool, confident manner gives the whole side a lift.*

"The understanding he has with Charlie George and George Armstrong over one-two's and free-kicks is uncanny.

"It makes me laugh when you still read people criticising this Arsenal side for so-called lack of flair. If George Graham doesn't have flair then we didn't do the double last season!"

Graham's success is all the more remarkable when you consider he joined Arsenal as a recognised striker in an attempt to end a woeful shortage of goals during their transitional period in 1966.

Yet Graham's inconsistency up front resulted in frequent speculation about his future. Matters came to a head during the

George Graham

▲ January 1972

1968-69 season when Graham found himself almost a permanent substitute. And with the development of talented teenagers like Charlie George and Ray Kennedy, the future looked bleak.

But then came a dramatic change of fortune with his switch to midfield. How does Graham explain the blossoming of his career?

He says: "Funnily enough, it was a complete accident. I was struggling to get into the side just before the League Cup Final with Swindon in 1969. I was substitute against Sheffield Wednesday at Hillsbrough when someone was injured. I was asked to drop back into midfield and did well in a 5-0 win. Since then I haven't looked back.

"I reckon I've got a lot of ball skill but up front you're restricted for space. Playing in the middle of the park has enabled me to show the ability I have. Up front you've nearly always got your back to goal and you can't see who's coming at you. Now I'm facing them and find I have the opportunity and time to be creative.

"What I found difficulty in adjusting to was the work-rate. The Arsenal lads have given me the nickname of "stroller" and quite honestly I don't like it.

"So apart from developing my ball skills I'm working much harder. I'm covering a lot of ground now whereas in the past I only came into the game in spasms.

"This led to a bit of friction last season when I was dropped for the Ipswich game at Portman Road. It made me realise that a player can have all the natural talent in the world but he won't get anywhere until he is prepared to be involved in a game for the full 90 minutes. I've overcome this problem now and would like to think I'm a better all-round player for it.

"What's more I haven't lost any of my old sharpness in front of goal. I got 14 last season in all competitions. Yet I still feel capable of getting more.

"One effort last season against Liverpool at Highbury pleased me no end. We were battling to break down their tough defence when I came on as a substitute. Within minutes I had taken a return pass from Jon Sammels and volleyed the ball past Ray Clemence."

Graham's high-level skills and midfield inspiration were rewarded in October when Scotland team manager Tommy Docherty called him up for the Nations Cup tie with Portugal at Hampden Park. Graham gave an impressive display and made the first goal for John O'Hare in a 2-1 win.

Graham was born in Bargeddie, a mining village seven miles from Glasgow and

Graham combines with Eddie Kelly for Arsenal's equaliser at Wembley

Aston Villa spotted him playing for Swinton, an amateur side in the West of Scotland League.

A Scottish Youth international, Graham was on Villa's books for four years and although he made two first-team appearances did not seem to fit in with their plans. Suddenly Graham found himself unwanted by a club who had finished fourth from bottom in the First Division in 1964.

Then Chelsea manager Tommy Docherty stepped in. After watching Graham play for the Rest of the United Kingdom against England in a special Youth match at Wembley, Docherty snapped him up for a give-away £6,000 in June, 1964.

When Graham arrived on the Stamford Bridge scene he was under no illusions about his future. He signed a two-year reserve contract which meant he was on lower wages than the men who made up the first-team pool.

Yet within months he had emerged as one of the most exciting young strikers in the game. And two months after the season's start his reserve-team contract was quickly scrapped and he was awarded a three-year first-team contract.

In his first season, 1964-65, he scored 17 League goals in 30 appearances and in the following season topped the Chelsea scoring chart with 23 first-team goals.

Ironically, Chelsea could have had him for nothing. As a 14-year-old Graham spent a month at Stamford Bridge during his school holidays. He decided not to return to London because he was homesick.

How is it then that Graham should hit it off at Chelsea? Says Graham: "The fact that Villa more or less wrote me off made me doubly determined to make the grade in London. When Joe Mercer let me go I was just 18 and I felt I was being thrown aside much too early. I vowed I would show Villa just how wrong they were."

Yet in 1966 an insuperable rift developed between the fiery Docherty and Graham which prompted several transfer requests. In September 1966 he moved across London to Highbury for £50,000 plus the £25,000-rated Tommy Baldwin after making just over 100 appearances for Chelsea.

Says Graham: "The move was the best thing that could have happened to me. While I owe Chelsea a great deal it was the Highbury set-up which really brought out the best in me.

"The present side has no weaknesses in any department. You name it and we've got it—flair, courage, strength—the lot. I see no reason why Arsenal shouldn't go on to even further honours, starting with the European Champions Cup. The boys would like to win that most for Bertie Mee."

If there was at any time any doubt about Graham's future then clearly everyone at Arsenal now realises he is an integral part of the Highbury system.

Graham's success story is a reflection of his character and determination to succeed and a perfect example to youngsters.

With courage and perseverance he has fought back twice to save a career, which, incredibly, seemed lost. It would have been a tragedy had that happened.

❛The fact that Villa wrote me off made me determined to make the grade❜ he told KEITH FISHER

MEET THE STARS . . .

England training at Roehampton is over for the day, but Arsenal's McNab won't be able to relax for quite a while yet judging by the crowd of young autograph-hunters closing in on him.

▲ 1971–72 Gift Book

CUP FINAL SPECIAL!

Last year's winner George Graham with his wife Marie and the Man-of-the-Match trophy

OUR MAN-OF-THE-MATCH

Graham (right) in action at Wembley

ALONG with the golden cup-winners' medal the "Football Monthly" Wembley Man-of-the-Match Award is the most coveted prize for any of the twenty-two players in the F.A. Cup Final at Wembley on May 6.

There is every possibility that the outstanding player and the winner of this magnificent trophy this year will be a defender. The law of averages point to a player in the defence receiving the award, for all three past winners have been forwards.

In 1969 it went to Allan Clarke, of Leicester City, after his great game against Manchester City. A year later he watched as his new Leeds United colleague Eddie Gray (Clarke had been transferred at the season's start) was presented with the award for a dazzling Wembley display against Chelsea. Both players had played on losing sides.

Then last year, that of the great Arsenal Cup and League double, a player on the winning team got the clear majority vote from the judges, the watching football journalists from all over the world . . .

George Graham, the subtle midfield provider, was a worthy winner of our Man-of-the-Match award, the imposing £500 silver trophy with its Wembley twin-towers prominent in a design which has won unanimous approval for originality and freshness of approach.

Like Allan Clarke and Eddie Gray, the canny Arsenal Scot has his Man-of-the-Match trophy as a magnificent memento of a proud day.

Who will win the award this year? *Will* it be a defender this time . . . a goalkeeper facing the odds, perhaps, or a dominating midfielder? A striking forward, one among the goals?

The three past winners have expressed their delight and appreciation of our unique reminder of football's most glamorous day, an award which lends even more excitement and anticipation to a wonderful sporting occasion.

Who will be the man-of-the-match this time? Football Monthly is waiting to salute him.

▲ April 1972

by KEITH FISHER

THE IMMENSE skills and sheer consistency of elegant defensive wing-half Peter Simpson were a rare delight in the disappointment of Arsenal's football last season. Acknowledged as one of the finest back-four players in the First Division, Simpson has helped forge the defensive authority which has acted as the club's springboard to success in recent years.

Yet Simpson did not receive the credit he was entitled to after Arsenal's nerve-wracking double-winning season in which he hardly misplaced a pass. And despite a decade at Highbury taking in nearly 300 first-team appearances, it was only last season that football folk began to realise the considerable contribution he makes each time he slips on that red-and-white jersey.

By defensive necessity, Simpson is not the kind of exciting eye-catching performer and his natural shyness is reflected in the way he prefers to remain overshadowed by more widely-known colleagues. Yet his qualities are fully appreciated by the men around him. He's dedicated, and his performances are stamped with the class of a thoroughbred professional.

Simpson tackles his job in the heart of the Arsenal defence with maximum efficiency and the minimum of fuss. He is a softly-spoken man whose modesty and affable off-field manner has endeared him to all at Highbury. And in an age when starry-eyed youngsters who haven't been in the game five minutes hold out their hands for cash before answering a few questions, it is refreshing to discover someone as unaffected by success as the down-to-earth Simpson.

❛ I don't mean to be rude, it's just that I get embarrassed talking to people ❜

It is strange now to recall that Simpson was once on offer to any interested club for a paltry £15,000. If there is a criticism to be levelled at this lean, angular defender it is in the self-doubts he harbours about his own ability. This was clearly illustrated during his teenage years at Highbury when he was on the verge of quitting the game.

First under George Swindin and then Billy Wright his progress was sound if not spectacular but it was not rapid enough to convince Peter that his future was in football. After a confrontation with Wright in 1965 he was slapped on the transfer list, clubs were circularised as to his availability, and there he remained for several months.

The unexpected promotion to manager of club physiotherapist Bertie Mee after the dismissal of Wright in 1966 was largely responsible for establishing the career of 21-year-old Peter Simpson at Arsenal. Mee, relatively unknown on the Soccer circuit but an expert in man-management from his time around the treatment-tables, told Simpson that if he made up his mind to

succeed he could be a fine player.

Their talk obviously cleared the inhibitions from Peter's mind. He set about tightening-up his game; he applied himself more diligently to training. Clearly, Mee gave Simpson the confidence he had been seeking and he has since blossomed into one of Highbury's most valuable assets.

A new defensive system of "zonal marking" introduced by former coach and assistant-manager Don Howe gave Simpson further proof of his unlimited potential.

Says Simpson: "As a youngster I was never really dedicated enough. I didn't care too much at all. It wasn't that I didn't have any ambition—I just believed I lacked the necessary ability to make the grade. I used to think to myself that I'd be best out of it all and settle down in some other career instead of facing an inevitable disappointment later on in life. I had no confidence.

"People are always telling me to have more assurance in myself. The boss keeps on at me for not pushing myself enough. But it's just not me. I've always been

quiet and like to keep myself to myself. After a match I prefer to avoid the reporters waiting in the foyer afterwards. I don't mean to be rude, it's just that I usually get embarrassed talking to people and half the time can't find anything to say. I like to prove myself on the pitch. That's where I earn my living.

"Possibly the biggest single influence on my career was marrying Ann. Now we have two children, both girls—Dan (5½) and Leh (2½)—live in a lovely house out in Cuffley in Hertfordshire, so what more can a fellow ask for? Above all, marriage gave me the determination to succeed. I had to sort myself out and the added responsibility was a key difference to my life."

In his early years, Simpson was regarded more for his useful ability as a "Jack of all trades" and this versatility earned him first-team spots in eight different positions. "I didn't like it at all," he says. "I was never settled. For five weeks I would be in at say full-back, then suddenly I was into midfield and I would have to keep on adapting my game.

"Then at the start of the 1967-68 season Don Howe started the zonal marking system where you mark a specific area instead of a particular individual. It had a great effect on my development as a player. I started off in pre-season training in the No. 6 shirt

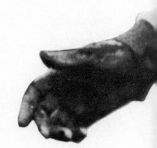

PETER SIMPSON

▲ June 1972

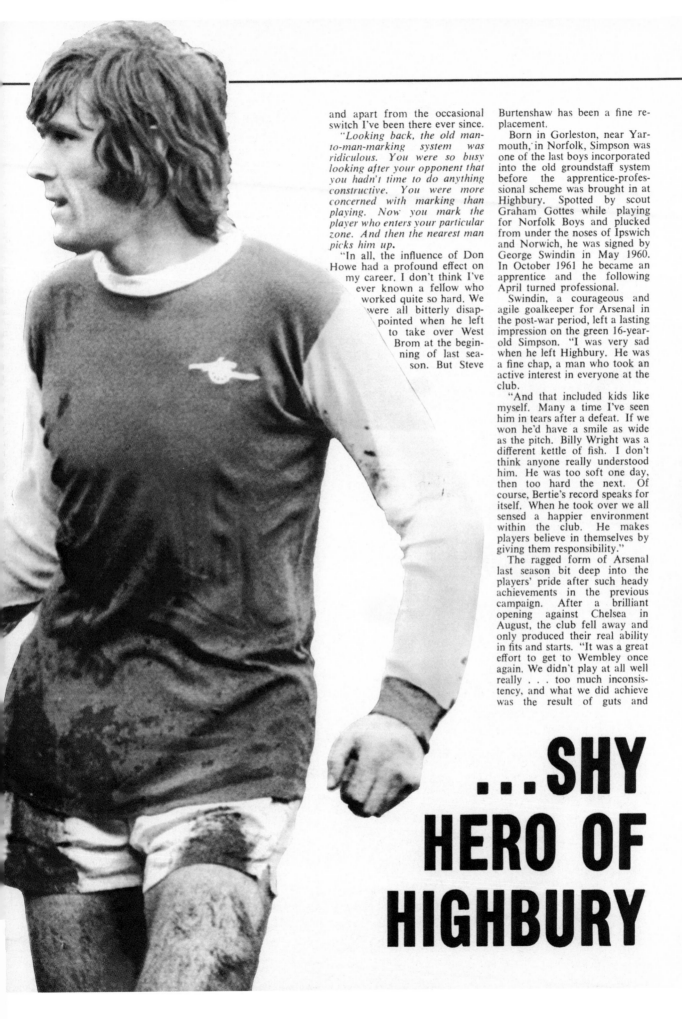

and apart from the occasional switch I've been there ever since.

"Looking back, the old man-to-man-marking system was ridiculous. You were so busy looking after your opponent that you hadn't time to do anything constructive. You were more concerned with marking than playing. Now you mark the player who enters your particular zone. And then the nearest man picks him up.

"In all, the influence of Don Howe had a profound effect on my career. I don't think I've ever known a fellow who worked quite so hard. We were all bitterly disappointed when he left to take over West Brom at the beginning of last season. But Steve Burtenshaw has been a fine replacement.

Born in Gorleston, near Yarmouth, in Norfolk, Simpson was one of the last boys incorporated into the old groundstaff system before the apprentice-professional scheme was brought in at Highbury. Spotted by scout Graham Gottes while playing for Norfolk Boys and plucked from under the noses of Ipswich and Norwich, he was signed by George Swindin in May 1960. In October 1961 he became an apprentice and the following April turned professional.

Swindin, a courageous and agile goalkeeper for Arsenal in the post-war period, left a lasting impression on the green 16-year-old Simpson. "I was very sad when he left Highbury. He was a fine chap, a man who took an active interest in everyone at the club.

"And that included kids like myself. Many a time I've seen him in tears after a defeat. If we won he'd have a smile as wide as the pitch. Billy Wright was a different kettle of fish. I don't think anyone really understood him. He was too soft one day, then too hard the next. Of course, Bertie's record speaks for itself. When he took over we all sensed a happier environment within the club. He makes players believe in themselves by giving them responsibility."

The ragged form of Arsenal last season bit deep into the players' pride after such heady achievements in the previous campaign. After a brilliant opening against Chelsea in August, the club fell away and only produced their real ability in fits and starts. "It was a great effort to get to Wembley once again. We didn't play at all well really . . . too much inconsistency, and what we did achieve was the result of guts and

...SHY HERO OF HIGHBURY

PETER SIMPSON

damned hard work. But even that must go some time. Obviously we suffered some reaction from our double triumph," he says.

Perhaps the biggest scar last season was the defeat by Ajax in the European Cup quarter-finals. Losing only 2-1 in Amsterdam gave Arsenal the confidence for an all-out assault in the return match at Highbury. But their dreams of winning the tournament at the first attempt were quickly dashed by a defensive error involving midfield man George Graham, who headed the ball into his own net in the 16th minute.

Simpson adds: "That we should be eliminated from the

George Swindin, then manager at Highbury, chats with Dave Bowen and Jack Kelsey. Frank McLintock (right) . . . great understanding with Simpson

competition by an own goal was sick. Our performance in Amsterdam was tremendous.

"Everyone ran until they dropped and although we lost, we felt it was a marvellous result for us. It was unfortunate for George Graham to give away that goal. He was inconsolable in the dressing-room afterwards. And so were we. It was like a morgue. This was the one we had been aiming for. But it was not to be."

Simpson was the victim of another own goal tragedy in the F.A. Cup semi-final against Stoke, but this time the Gunners survived, despite the loss of goalkeeper Bob Wilson, to again reach Wembley by the replay route.

Until Arsenal won the European Fairs Cup in 1970, the club was recognised more for its glorious past than an ambitious future. Their last domestic success was in 1953 when they carried off the Football League Championship. "When I joined the club everyone kept reminding the lads what the club had achieved in the 30s and 40s. The ghosts of Alex James and company were finally buried with the breakthrough of that Fairs Cup victory. It was an enormous relief and we have gone on from there.

"Yet even now the critics won't get off our back. There was the inevitable comparison with the Super Spurs of 1961. People say we haven't got flair and that our football is too rigid and stereotyped. It's quite ridiculous really. What about players like Charlie George, George Graham and George Armstrong? I'll admit that basically we are a hard-working side but in today's football no team can succeed without defensive organisation.

"One of the biggest factors in our success was that the team had practically grown up together. The youth team I played in at Arsenal contained Peter Storey, George Armstrong, Jon Sammels and David Court. Frank McLintock has been here since 1964, George Graham since 1966 and Bob Wilson since 1963. And with lads like Eddie Kelly, Charlie George, Ray Kennedy and Pat Rice coming through the youth channel we all knew each other's games inside out, which fostered a tremendous team atmosphere.

"One thing we found out last season was that teams no longer underestimate Arsenal. Far from it. Everyone was out to whip the Champions. A side needs a tremendous amount of luck to win anything. In our Double year if we had two shots at goal they both went in. Last season they went wide. After clinching all the honours against Liverpool at Wembley I just felt

like a cabbage—drained of all emotion. It only began to sink in on a close season holiday in Torremolinos which the club arranged for us. Then we began to realise we had achieved the impossible.

Simpson's almost telepathic understanding with skipper Frank McLintock has developed into one of the most successful defensive partnerships in the London club's history. The experienced McLintock switched to the centre-half spot three years ago from a more taxing midfield role.

Alongside the dependable Simpson, McLintock found a new lease of life in his more subdued role and the pair struck an immediate and perfect working relationship. And this success is all the more creditable when you realise Simpson is only 5 ft. 10 in. and his captain 5 ft. 9 in., hardly the traditional sizes for such a demanding job.

"Frank has this tremendous ability to read a game and with his natural enthusiasm makes the ideal leader. He's the boss on and off the field," says Simpson. "On it he's always talking and cajoling players into more effort, off the field he's always looking after the players' interests and he's always ready to help a player if he's not getting enough money."

Simpson has gone into business, converting houses into flats, which ensures a healthy financial future once his playing days are over. At 27, he is realistic enough to admit that any England ambitions have gone right out of his head. "There was a time when perhaps I used to give it a lot of thought. Sir Alf Ramsey called me into a couple of squads during the 1968-69 season and I was selected for the original 1970 World Cup squad."

In typical fashion, he adds: "Let's be honest, the way Bobby Moore is playing he could go on until he is 40. And with up-and-coming youngsters like Colin Todd and Jeff Blockley I can't see much chance of getting a look-in.

"I've experienced four Wembley finals and won a League Championship and Fairs Cup Winners' medal so life can't be bad. And you can't help but envisage an exciting future for Arsenal. Half the squad are under 25 and have already been weaned on success. I just hope I can continue to be part of a successful side."

Clearly, Simpson has proved he is an integral part of the Arsenal set-up. And with his permanency at left-half has come a real assurance in his play. In the meantime, the "quiet one" of Highbury will continue to give 100 per cent effort every time he sets foot on the pitch.

PAT RICE
Arsenal

FAMILY ALBUM

P-r-e-s-e-n-t-i-n-g . . . Paul
Marinello! He's the five-months-old
son of Joyce and Peter, the Arsenal's
Scottish forward and there's no
doubting here that Mum and Dad
are real proud of their wee lad

▲ November 1972

DECEMBER 1972 20p
USA $1·20
S AFRICA   60c
NIGERIA   4/-

football

MONTHLY

A study in concentration as
Arsenal striker John Radford
shields the ball from Leicester
City defender Malcolm Manley

MARTIN BUCHAN
IN GIANT COLOUR

Aston Villa's
Amiable
Andy

George Armstrong

THEY JUST WIND HIM UP AND OFF HE GOES!

▲ June 1973

His all-action, all-out style sometimes under-sells Highbury's amazing little man but the people who should know, managers and the stars themselves, give the thumbs-up sign for Arsenal's long-serving winger. Here he talks to KEITH FISHER about the big moments—and the bad

A METER attached to George Armstrong's busy little legs to record his fantastic mileage during a normal 90 minutes, would make the fans begin to realise the immense contribution he has made to Arsenal's success.

Armstrong, who never knows when to give in, is a player managers need to cure the insomnia and insecurity of their profession. Determined and unselfish, he never shirks a challenge and combines his wing skills with a tireless enthusiasm that enables him to chase and harry opponents into all kinds of error in midfield.

It is a style unique in many ways. He can follow any rigid tactical formation, yet still retain the individualism and flair which marks him as one of the most dangerous wingers in the business.

Born in Hebburn, Co. Durham—hence his affectionate nickname "Geordie" —Armstrong first linked with Highbury back in 1961. The Gunners longest-serving professional, his 450-plus League appearances have been characterised by the sweat and honest-to-goodness effort he has given in their cause.

Chelsea manager Dave Sexton summed it all up after watching his side fall to Arsenal in the FA Cup Sixth Round after two throbbing, keenly contested matches. He said: "If I have to pick out someone for particular mention then it must be Armstrong. This fellow never stops running and working for his team-mates. *His performances were out of this world.*"

That assessment is backed up by Armstrong's many admirers. Manchester United captain Bobby Charlton says: "He has gone from strength to strength, working hard and taking weight off defenders' shoulders by his willingness to get back and help out."

Chris Lawler, the Liverpool full-back, suitably qualified to sum up Armstrong's game after their exciting struggles over the years adds: 'He possesses this fantastic will-to-win and once he's got the ball it's very difficult to make him part with it. He roams all over the place and he's such a nimble fellow."

Now listen to Malcolm

Armstrong gives Liverpool defenders Chris Lawler and Ray Clemence an anxious moment during the 1971 FA Cup Final at Wembley, where Arsenal clinched the coveted "double".

Allison, not exactly noted for his tact in dealing with players' capabilities. "His uncanny ability to time and present the perfect cross, his elusiveness and most of all his sheer stamina has been a deciding force for the Gunners."

Back at Highbury and £200,000 centre-half Jeff Blockley admits he has been amazed at Armstrong's energy. "When I was at Coventry I always rated George but it's only when you play with him that you realise just what a great player he is. The minute he steps out on to the pitch he starts running and doesn't stop."

Last but not least, over to Arsenal skipper Frank McLintock. The craggy Scot says: "Last season he had a great time. Yet the point is that he's been playing like that for many years but it's only now that people have come round to realising his worth. *He's hardly had a mention, even during our double year.*

"George is the type of player who just gets on with

the job and the fans tend to take him for granted. You only start to miss him, it seems, when he's out of the side. His stamina is phenomenal. He's just as energetic during training.

"After a hard match some of us may come to the ground feeling whacked the following morning, but George never tires. We cannot understand where he gets it all from. We'd all like to know the secret. But above all, he's such a popular wee man with everybody. He's always got a smile on his face."

Yet put the question of his incredible stamina to the man himself and he genuinely cannot understand all the fuss. Says George: "It's something I never think about. Some players have marvellous skills, like Alan Ball, and they can practically do anything with the ball. Others are really gritty and can tackle like demons.

"My game is built on running, but I reckon there are other Arsenal players who do just as much as me. Perhaps it's my short legs that make me stand out!"

The prime illustration of Armstrong's effect on the side was seen last season. After playing in Arsenal's first seven matches, he then injured a knee and while out of action in stepped Peter Marinello. "Geordie" couldn't recapture his old spot.

Yet during his absence Arsenal showed indifferent form and it all blew up in their faces in November after their inglorious 3-0 exit from the Football League Cup quarter-finals at the hands of First Division babes Norwich City and then the humiliation of a 5-0 defeat by Derby at the Baseball Ground three days later.

Recalls Armstrong: "Bertie Mee called us in for an emergency team-meeting that Sunday and both he and coach Steve Burtenshaw encouraged us to express our feelings to the full. It was certainly the frankest discussion I've experienced in my time at Highbury. But the important thing was that it was open and honest.

"It enabled us to get everything off our chest and it proved very successful. We

GEORGE ARMSTRONG

all agreed that we had to get down to basics again. We started the season adopting a new style of ambitious Soccer similar to that of Ajax, of Holland. It began really well and I don't think anyone who watched our 5-2 thrashing of Wolves early on would disagree.

"But while we had become more entertaining in trying to cut out the long balls to the big men up front we lost a lot of steel and determination in our approach and couldn't really reach any consistency.

"It was decided to revert to the old policy and after that our results spoke for themselves. People say that having only a twin spearhead makes us stereotyped and predictable, allowing the opposition to easily counter our build-up.

"The difference is that Ray Kennedy and John Radford are so good and present so many problems that no defence can know what to expect next."

Armstrong's recall to the No. 7 jersey coincided with a run of 18 unbeaten matches before Albion emerged with a 1-0 success at the Hawthorns in March. It also meant the London club coming under severe criticism once again for their so-called negative attitudes. It's a point that makes the little man see red.

"No matter how successful Arsenal are it seems they will always be under fire. People say we're dull and unattractive, but just ask any Arsenal regular what he thinks. WINNING is an entertainment and people wouldn't watch us otherwise. With all the talk last season of dropping attendances just compare our gates and there is very little difference.

"When you consider we have players like Ball, Charlie George, Radford and Eddie Kelly it's hard to believe that few give us any credit for our football. But we just let our points total do the talking for us."

Armstrong mellows considerably when discussing his own role in the Gunners revival. "I honestly thought I played some of the best stuff of my career when I got back into the side. Playing in the reserves week after week is murder.

Former Arsenal boss George Swindin (above) who signed Armstrong in 1961. Right: Pat Rice, one of the Gunners' many home-grown products and Alan Ball (opposite page), who has a added new dimension to their play

"There's no atmosphere and incentive to play well. It had an effect on my home life too, and I must have been pretty unbearable with the wife and kids. One of the worst things is when you look at the next fixture, say against Manchester City, and it sinks in that you will not be playing.

"I've never felt more depressed in my career. You snap at everyone and just sit and think of what to do next. I don't want to go through all that again. I was fortunate in that both Ray Kennedy and Peter Simpson were in the reserves with me and I suppose we could drown our sorrows together!

"It got to such a state that I went in to have a chat with Bertie Mee. He said that I'd be at Highbury as long as he was, but Peter Marinello had waited three years for his chance and I'd have to grit my teeth and work doubly hard to get back in.

"There was no question of a transfer. I admire the club too much for that. I've more or less grown up here. When I got back I was determined to do well. You've got to because we have such a strong pool of players that one bad game and you are on the sidelines again!

"But I just seemed to re-

capture all my old zest and enthusiasm for the game and when the side's going well it makes you push a bit harder. Mind you, I couldn't have had a more difficult start. We played Leeds at Highbury in my first game and then faced our biggest rivals, Spurs, at White Hart Lane. We won both and I didn't look back. I've never felt more keyed-up to do well.

"Take our Cup replay against Chelsea. At first I couldn't get into the ground, there were so many fans queueing up that all the entrances were blocked. At that moment I sensed it would be our night.

"I had butterflies in my stomach hours before the start and was just itching to get cracking. That must rate as one of the best performances of my career."

After his lung-busting efforts last season, it is strange now to recall that Armstrong has twice been on the verge of leaving Highbury and on reflection Bertie Mee must be mighty thankful that nothing emerged from these unsettling periods.

A complete loss of form back in 1966 which resulted in him being dropped for a lengthy spell prompted

Armstrong to slap in a transfer-request.

He says: "I never really wanted to go, but I wasn't achieving anything on the field and being a little immature asked for a move. It all blew up when I went storming in to see Dave Sexton to have a real barney. He just let me go on and on and when I'd said my piece he simply pointed out that I was kidding myself and the way I was playing I would get nowhere fast. I knew he was right."

That wasn't the end of his troubles. Just three years later he became even more convinced that he had no future at the club when first Jimmy Robertson arrived in a swop deal which took Dave Jenkins to Spurs, then Bertie Mee splashed £100,000 on Hibernian winger Peter Marinello and he was slowly edged out of the first-team reckoning.

Then came a dramatic swing in events . . .

He came on as substitute during the first-leg clash with Ajax in the European Fairs Cup semi-finals with the score standing at 1-0 and immediately had a hand in two more goals to enable the Gunners to build up a com-

manding advantage. He kept his place for the return in Amsterdam and was one of the stars on a night when Arsenal's superb defensive performance resisted all the pressure of the skilful Dutch team.

Armstrong left his most impressive display for the final against Anderlecht at Highbury when his weaving runs and unceasing effort singled him out as the man of the match.

Arsenal, facing a 3-1 deficit from the first match in Brussels, roared to a 3-0 triumph and gained their first major honour for 17 years.

It didn't stop there and no player worked harder than Armstrong in helping to land the coveted "double" next season.

He was an ever-present in all competitions, taking in a total of 64 matches, and was voted "Player of the Year" by the Arsenal Supporters' Club.

Adds George: "When I look back that Fairs Cup success was a make or break time for me. Luckily, anything I tried came off. It seemed my face didn't fit and I went out to prove them wrong. Since then life couldn't have been better.

"I've always said that to win a League Championship medal would be my one big ambition in football, but to get both honours in one season was too good to be true. After clinching the title at Spurs someone turned round and told us not to overdo the celebrations as we had another important match to play. 'It's only the Cup Final' we all choroused—and got back to sipping the champagne!"

What has been the formula behind Arsenal's leap to the top? "Possibly the fact that most of us have been together since we were kids," he says. "I joined the club at the same time as Peter Storey and played in a youth side containing Peter Simpson, Jon Sammels and David Court. We have all been together so long now that we know each other inside out.

"Take youngsters like Charlie George, Eddie Kelly, Pat Rice, Ray Kennedy and Sammy Nelson. They have been at Highbury since leaving school. No wonder we possess such a tremendous team-spirit."

Armstrong is quick to acknowledge the debt they owe former coaches Dave Sexton and Don Howe. "Dave was a master at making football seem simple and put a lot of enjoyment into our game. Don Howe made us into a great side. He organised the defence to act as our springboard to success and it just developed from there.

"What rankles with the players is that Bertie Mee hardly receives any credit for what he has achieved at Arsenal. He has a tremendous record and his ability at picking the right men for the right job stands out a mile."

"Geordie" is one of a family of nine children, seven boys and two girls. Like most local lads he had ambitions of joining Newcastle United and although he spent two weeks at St. James's Park he was allowed to slip through their net.

He returned to his job as an apprentice electrician and took up where he left off in Durham Junior Soccer. On the recommendation of Arsenal's chief northern representative, he was invited to London for trials in the spring of 1961.

Originally an inside-forward, it was former manager George Swindin who spotted his immense potential as a winger and snapped him up as a professional after just two days! His progress was so swift that within the space of months he had secured a regular first-team place at 17.

He retains many warm memories of his start under Swindin. "George was a terrific fellow who really looked after you. He was a real boss. If you turned up late for training he'd be waiting at the end of the corridor to give you a back-hander around the ear!

"But he was such a warm person. I remember after making my debut against Blackpool when we won 1-0 and I laid on the goal for Geoff Strong he came running up to me and said "Bloody marvellous, son." As a youngster those words meant the world to me. It was a very sad day for me when he left."

How has Armstrong's style remained unaffected in the wingless era since the World Cup success of 1966 . . . or can he be specifically labelled as a winger?

"Put it this way," he says. "When Arsenal are attacking my role is to get behind defenders on the wing. Of course, when we are under pressure I like to help out by challenging for possession in midfield. I've got to be involved all the time so I reckon that's where the 'run-run-run' tag comes in."

In which ways has the game changed during his time? "For a start there are no more dud full-backs," he adds regretfully! "There were always a few defenders you could turn it on against. They'd still be on their backside after you had put over a cross.

"There is much more skill in every position. The side I first played in contained one of the best forward-lines in the game—Johnny MacLeod, Geoff Strong, Joe Baker, George Eastham and myself. We used to score a hatful of goals but still lose 5-4 because we gave so many goals away at the back! That was Arsenal all over, erratic but very exciting to watch. *Some of us have nightmares re-living those games.*"

Armstrong believes the arrival of Alan Ball has added a new dimension to their play. "Alan has been so good for us and given more variety and confidence going forward. He was in tremendous form last season. The annoying thing is that so many critics were calling us 'lucky' after nearly every game. The fact that we managed to come from behind to get results surely is a reflection of our never-say-die attitude. There is a lot of character in this team. I've been too long in this game to expect anything handed on a plate. You make your own luck."

In August, he celebrates his 29th birthday and he is confident of a good many years football left in him. "I feel on top of the world and as soon as the season ended I was already beginning to look forward to another. I have always been a good trainer and kept myself in peak condition. *The way I'm playing now I could go on till I was 40. I'm going to have a try!*"

With an eye on the future he has invested money into a company that deals with the development of blocks of flats, but he is quick to point out: "I never let it interfere with my football. I'm a great believer in living only for today and letting tomorrow look after itself. I never look on football as a business but something that gives me endless pleasure. I enjoy every moment of it."

It is this happy-go-lucky approach which has endeared him to everyone at Highbury. Wee Georgie Armstrong so clearly RELISHES dragging every ounce of energy from his body as he buzzes non-stop around the field.

I wish it could be said of the majority of our stars.

£220,000 for A. Ball!

Alan Ball, repeat Alan Ball, wait at Watford to meet an Arsenal official

A call home to wife Lesley while they wait

Now it can be told . . . Arsenal manager Bertie Mee wears an expensive smile, Ball waits for the next question from the Press

▲ 1973–74 Gift Book

Here's Alan's home debut—against Everton! And a few lads who can boast that they had their hands on big money for a moment

THERE were just three days to Christmas when Arsenal went shopping and bought a Ball, and the bill totted up to £220,000, biggest-ever British transfer fee. But before Alan, of Everton, left his native northern parts he, like any dutiful son, asked Dad's advice. Dad, being himself a manager—of Preston North End —and a responsible parent, went along to see what prospects there were in the new job at Highbury, came away satisfied there was every chance of good wages and promotion and young Alan has not looked back since taking the job

S.G.B.

Postscript

In May 2005, Alan Ball, the subject of our final extract from the Charles Buchan archive, put up for auction various memorabilia from his playing days, most notably his World Cup winner's medal, in order to raise cash for his grandchildren. A year earlier Ball's wife had died from cancer. His daughter had also been diagnosed with the disease. The sale raised £140,000.

Two years later, in April 2007, the 61 year old Ball, who had enjoyed a chequered career as a manager since retiring, and who was awarded an MBE in 2000, suffered from a fatal heart attack.

The private lives of footballers after they have hung up their boots have long held an almost ghoulish fascination for the public, and although following the abolition of the maximum wage in 1961 most players fared better than their predecessors, the words of Herbert Chapman still ring true today. Of the newly retired footballer, Chapman wrote (shortly before his own death – see page 143), 'The bottom has dropped out of his world. He feels he must do something to make a fresh start and, perhaps without proper advice, he plunges into an undertaking which fails.

'Such a man deserves pity.'

Jimmy Logie's last game for Arsenal was in 1954. Said the judge at his appearance before a bankruptcy court five years later, 'It seems that he was a better footballer than businessman.'

Happily, Logie reconstructed his life, and dabbled more successfully in the pub trade. But for many Arsenal fans the abiding image of Logie was of him selling newspapers in Piccadilly Circus. A heavy gambler, he later admitted, 'I drank more than I should have done in order to blot out the depression of my playing career finishing.'

Logie died in 1984, aged 64.

Another former Arsenal star whose later business ventures failed to bring him security was Tommy Lawton, as a result of which one of his former clubs, Everton, laid on a testimonial match in 1972. After he died in 1996 his ashes were presented to the National Football Museum in Preston.

A common career for ex-players to follow in the days of *Charles Buchan's Football Monthly* was that of publican. Vic Groves followed this path before building a career in insurance. 'It takes a while,' he later admitted, 'but if you can accept that the football side of your life is over – and move on – then eventually other things will fill the void.' His great nephew Perry Groves played for Arsenal in the late 1980s.

Geoff Strong, sold to Liverpool in 1964, co-owned a pub with a former Anfield colleague, Ian Callaghan, before setting up a furnishing business. Dennis Evans became a chauffeur. Joe Baker, sold to Forest, then to Sunderland, also became a publican, in Scotland, while after a brief swansong at Luton, Danny Clapton ran a pub in Hackney. In June 1986 he was found dead in his home on Penshurst Road. He was 51.

In common with many a former Gunner, Clapton sampled life overseas, playing for a brief period in Sydney. Gordon Nutt followed, ending up in the Australian film industry, where his most enduring credit was as assistant director on the cult 1974 movie, *Stone*.

George Eastham, forever known as the player who challenged the retain and transfer system in 1963, and awarded an OBE a decade later, spent seven years at Stoke before emigrating to South Africa in 1978. There he defied apartheid by coaching black and coloured players. In 2007 he was a guest of honour at the Professional Footballers' Association centenary celebrations. Yet he still felt it neccessary to auction his 1966 England shirt to help pay for his daughter's education.

After leaving Arsenal in 1960 for Blackburn, Millwall and Bristol Rovers, Joe Haverty crossed the Atlantic to play in Chicago, Kansas City and Dallas, before retiring with Shelbourne back in Ireland. 'Playing for Arsenal gave me the chance to travel, which I think is more important than having money in the bank,' Haverty later said. Subsequently he became a welder for Volkswagen, whilst also doing some scouting work for Arsenal.

Cliff Holton moved around too, playing at five other lower division clubs and scoring freely at each before hanging up his boots in 1968 to work in engineering.

Of all that generation Jack Kelsey moved the least, taking up a job in Arsenal's commercial department, where he remained until his death in 1992. 'A lot of players laboured under the misunderstanding that they'd be given a job with clubs after they retired,' Kelsey once commented. 'And most ended up heartbroken. I was one of the lucky ones, because in my role in the shop many people still wanted to talk football, which helped to fill the void which all ex-players still feel on match day. That never leaves you – the missing out on the fun and the camaraderie.'

Some filled that void by going into club management.

After eight successful seasons at Manchester United and Stoke, David Herd went on to manage Waterford (in Ireland) and Lincoln City. Lionel Smith spent six years as manager of Gravesend and Northfleet. Joe Wade enjoyed success at Hereford, before opening a sports shop. Gerry Ward ended up as manager at Barnet, while George Swindin of course served his managerial apprenticeship at Peterborough before being elevated to the hot seat at Highbury. After resigning in 1962 Swindin went on to manage Norwich, Cardiff, Kettering and finally Corby, where he eventually owned a garage.

Dave Bowen's long spell as manager of Northampton Town included their meteoric rise from the Fourth to the First Divisions between 1961–65. One of his successors was another Highbury contemporary, Bill Dodgin, who also managed at QPR, Fulham and Brentford. Another Gunner-turned-manager was Jimmy Bloomfield, boss at Orient and Leicester.

But most successful of all the 1950s crew was Joe Mercer.

Having signed for Arsenal as a stop gap in 1946 the genial Mercer ended up playing 246 games for the Gunners before embarking on a managerial career that took in Sheffield United, Aston Villa and, for a brief spell, a caretaker role for the England team. In 1968 he led Manchester City to the First Division title, followed by victory in the FA Cup a year later (thus he become one of the few men to lift the Cup both as a player and manager). He was awarded an OBE in 1976.

Mercer lived to the age of 76. But all too many of his contemporaries died younger; Jim Fotheringham at the age of 43, Jimmy Bloomfield at 49, and the majority of the others mentioned above, like Alan Ball, in their sixties.

'It's no surprise that footballers from my era don't live to a particularly old age,' said Derek Tapscott, referring to the damage incurred from heading the old style heavy footballs. 'It's a wonder any of us have any brain cells left.'

Tapscott's own playing career ended with spells at Cardiff and Newport, after which he worked for the boot manufacturers, Gola.

And what of Boys Club member 1470, featured in May 1959?

Peter Goy, *Soccer Boy of the Month* in March 1952, ended up playing only two first team games for Arsenal. But he spent five years with Southend, Watford and Huddersfield, before establishing a business in Rayleigh, Essex, printing stickers for football clubs.

Of the 1960s generation, after finishing his career at Leicester City, Jon Sammels ran a driving school in Leicestershire. Peter Simpson slipped back to the anonymity he craved in his native Norfolk, running a garage business, and later the bar at a nearby golf club. John Radford, who currently works in the corporate area at the Emirates Stadium, also chauffeurs in Hertfordshire, having spent several years managing non-League Bishops Stortford, while Sammy Nelson became an insurance broker.

After eleven seasons at Highbury Terry Neill shocked everyone by moving from Hull City to become manager of arch rivals Tottenham in 1974. Even more surprisingly two years later he was appointed as Bertie Mee's successor, thereby becoming Arsenal's youngest ever manager at the age of 34. Bertie Mee spent the rest of his career at Watford and was made an OBE in 1984. Neill did reasonably well in seven years at Highbury but then left to run a sports bar in Holborn.

Bob McNab settled in Los Angeles, where he became a property developer. (His daughter Mercedes starred in the television series *Buffy the Vampire Slayer*.)

Peter Storey's career took a rather different turn. Two years after the last of his 387 games for Arsenal, the tough midfielder was convicted for running a brothel in east London. A succession of prison terms followed, for counterfeiting, car theft and the importing of pornography. Storey subsequently settled in France.

Post-football life for Peter Marinello was to prove similarly challenging, shattering the image of the happy family man depicted in the November 1972 issue.

Twice Marinello was declared bankrupt. Once he was arrested for threatening to murder a former business partner. For years he lived as a virtual down-and-out, whilst his son became a heroin addict

and his wife succumbed to severe depression. Now living in Dorset and acting as a full time carer for former model Joyce, he claims, 'Even if I'd earned £100,000 a week, I still reckon that I'd have contrived to lose it.' His autobiography *Fallen Idle* (see page 143) makes the tabloid confessions of fellow Scot Alex James seem innocent in the extreme.

Just as James and the stars of the 1930s continued to visit Highbury long after their playing days were over, so Marinello can still be seen at occasional Arsenal home games, as can Charlie George, a regular match day host.

George, who has also worked as a car mechanic, admits that he spent his riches as quickly as he earned them. Yet as an Islington boy his popularity amongst Arsenal fans has never faded, and he seldom tires of giving differing accounts of why he did his famous impression of Jesus Christ Superstar after scoring the winner in the 1971 FA Cup Final.

Other members of the 1970–71 Double winning squad have remained firmly in the limelight.

Frank McLintock, awarded an MBE in 1972, made little impression as a manager at either Leicester or Brentford, and in 1997 was implicated in a much publicised 'bungs' enquiry into his role as an agent in the transfer of Teddy Sheringham from Nottingham Forest to Spurs. He has since carved a successful career as a pundit for Sky Sports. Goalkeeper Bob Wilson went further, becoming a regular anchorman for BBC television's *Football Focus* and then for ITV's match coverage, until his retirement in 2002.

But undoubtedly the most battle scarred of all former Gunners to have entered television punditry has been George Graham.

After serving his coaching apprenticeship at Crystal Palace and QPR, Graham became manager

at Millwall, before taking on the Arsenal job in 1986. Over the next nine years the man once dubbed as Stroller for his laid back approach on the field led a disciplined Arsenal to two League titles, two League Cup victories, an FA Cup win and the European Cup Winners Cup. And yet instead of going down in history as one of Arsenal's greatest ever managers, he left the club under a cloud in 1995 following allegations that he had accepted illegal payments from a Norwegian agent. (After a one year ban he returned to management with Leeds and, surprisingly, Tottenham.)

Two of Graham's contemporaries also returned to Arsenal. George Armstrong spent ten years as a coach until his sudden death from a brain haemorrhage, incurred at the club's Colney Hatch training ground. He was 56.

Working alongside Armstrong was Pat Rice, appointed youth team coach in 1984. Following in the footsteps of Tom Whittaker and Jack Crayston, since 1996 Rice has fulfilled the role of assistant manager (to Arsene Wenger).

Finally, for Ray Kennedy, life after Highbury brought mixed blessings. After joining Liverpool in 1974 he won a glut of honours, European and domestic. Then at the age of 35 Kennedy was diagnosed with Parkinson's disease. A library in his name is held at the Parkinson's Disease Society in London, and when able, he works hard to raise awareness of this crippling ailment. Like Alan Ball, he too was forced to sell all his caps, medals and memorabilia in order to stay afloat.

And so for the players of the 1950s and '60s, fortune has dealt a mixed hand; contentment and riches for some, disappointment and hardship for others. But in one respect, along with Charlie Buchan they share at least one common bond, and that is a place, however large or small, in the remarkable history of Arsenal Football Club.

MEET THE PLAYERS ▶

Index

Further reading

Allison, George *Allison Calling – A Galaxy of Football and Other Memories* Staples Press (1948)
Ball, Alan *It's All About A Ball* WH Allen (1978)
Barnes, Wally *Captain of Wales – Wally Barnes* Stanley Paul (1953)
Buchan, Charles *A Lifetime in Football* Phoenix House (1955)
Chapman, Herbert *Herbert Chapman on Football* Garrick Publishing (1934)
Compton, Dennis *End of an Innings* Oldbourne (1958)
Eastham, George *Determined to Win* Stanley Paul (1964)
George, Charlie *My Story* Century (2005)
Graham, George *The Glory and the Grief: The Life of George Graham* Andre Deutsch (1996)
Harding, John *Alex James, Life of a Football Legend* Robson Books (1988)
Harris, Jeff and Hogg, Tony (ed) *Arsenal Who's Who* Independent UK Sports (1995)
Inglis, Simon (ed) *The Best of Charles Buchan's Football Monthly* English Heritage (2006)
James, Gary *Football With A Smile – the Authorised Biography of Joe Mercer* ACL & Polar (1993)
Kelsey, Jack and Glanville, Brian *Over the Bar – Jack Kelsey* Stanley Paul (1958)
Kennedy, Ray and Lees, Andrew *Ray of Hope: The Ray Kennedy Story* Pelham (1993)
King, Jeff and Willis, Tony *George Graham – The Wonder Years* Virgin (1995)
Lawton, Tommy *When The Cheering Stopped – The Rise, The Fall* Golden Eagle (1973)
McLintock, Frank and MacNeill, Terry *That's the Way the Ball Bounces* Pelham (1969)
McLintock, Frank *True Grit – Frank McLintock – The Autobiography* Headline 2006
Marinello, Peter *Fallen Idle – Fighting Back from the Booze, Swindles and Drugs That Ripped My Life Apart* Headline (2007)
Neill, Terry *Revelations of a Football Manager* Sidgwick & Jackson (1985)
Sammels, Jon and Oxby, Robert *Double Champions – Playing the Arsenal Way* Arthur Barker (1971)
Soar, Phil and Tyler, Martin *Arsenal 1886-1986 – The Official Centenary History* Hamlyn (1986)
Spurling, Jon *Highbury – The Story of Arsenal in N5* Orion Books (2005)
Spurling, Jon *Rebels for the Cause: The Alternative History of Arsenal Football Club* Mainstream (2004)
Studd, Stephen *Herbert Chapman – Football Emperor* Peter Owen (1981)
Taylor, Graham *Bertie Mee: Arsenal's Officer and Gentleman* Mainstream (2005)
Ure, Ian *Ure's Truly* Pelham (1968)
Wall, Bob *Arsenal from the Heart* Souvenir Press (1969)
Whittaker, Tom and Peskett, Roy *Tom Whittaker's Arsenal Story* Sporting Handbooks (1957)
Wilson, Bob *Behind the Network – My Autobiography* Coronet (2004)

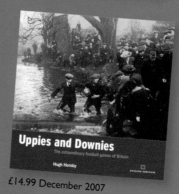

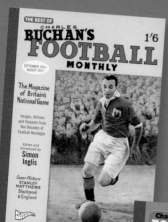
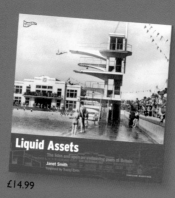

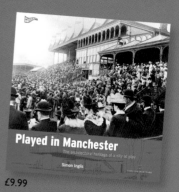